Cambridge Elements ≡

Elements in the Aegean Bronze Age
edited by
Carl Knappett
University of Toronto
Irene Nikolakopoulou
Hellenic Ministry of Culture and Archaeological Museum of Heraklion

LONG-DISTANCE EXCHANGE AND INTER-REGIONAL ECONOMIES

Sarah C. Murray
University of Toronto

CAMBRIDGE
UNIVERSITY PRESS

CAMBRIDGE
UNIVERSITY PRESS

Shaftesbury Road, Cambridge CB2 8EA, United Kingdom

One Liberty Plaza, 20th Floor, New York, NY 10006, USA

477 Williamstown Road, Port Melbourne, VIC 3207, Australia

314–321, 3rd Floor, Plot 3, Splendor Forum, Jasola District Centre, New Delhi – 110025, India

103 Penang Road, #05–06/07, Visioncrest Commercial, Singapore 238467

Cambridge University Press is part of Cambridge University Press & Assessment, a department of the University of Cambridge.

We share the University's mission to contribute to society through the pursuit of education, learning and research at the highest international levels of excellence.

www.cambridge.org
Information on this title: www.cambridge.org/9781009478595

DOI: 10.1017/9781009319188

First published 2023

A catalogue record for this publication is available from the British Library

ISBN 978-1-009-47859-5 Hardback
ISBN 978-1-009-31917-1 Paperback
ISSN 2754-2998 (online)
ISSN 2754-298X (print)

Long-Distance Exchange and Inter-Regional Economies

Elements in the Aegean Bronze Age

DOI: 10.1017/9781009319188
First published online: December 2023

Sarah C. Murray
University of Toronto

Author for correspondence: Sarah C. Murray, sc.murray@utoronto.ca

Abstract: An undulating flow of multiscalar exchanges pulsed across the surface of the Aegean from the beginnings of the Bronze Age in the third millennium to the transition into the Iron Age nearly 2,000 years later. Such exchanges were variable in nature. Most of these exchanges probably occurred within a rather circumscribed environment, involving neighboring communities operating across the many real but traversable geographical boundaries that characterize the Aegean landscape – ridges separating mountain plateaus, rocky coastal stretches between bays, or narrow straits amidst archipelagos. This Element is focused on the less-frequent but important long-distance exchanges that connected people in the Aegean with the wider Mediterranean and European world, especially focusing on interactions that may be classified as "economic." After reviewing basic definitions and discussing some methods and materials available for studying long-distance exchange, this Element presents a diachronic assessment of the geospatial, scalar, and structural characteristics of long-distance exchange and interregional economies.

Keywords: Bronze Age economics, prehistoric exchange systems, maritime trade, Aegean Bronze Age, political geography

ISBNs: 9781009478595 (HB), 9781009319171 (PB), 9781009319188 (OC)
ISSNs: 2754-2998 (online), 2754-298X (print)

Contents

1 Introduction

An undulating flow of multiscalar exchanges pulsed across the surface of the Aegean from the beginning of the Bronze Age in the third millennium until the transition to the Iron Age nearly two thousand years later. Such exchanges were variable in nature. Most probably occurred within a rather circumscribed environment, involving neighboring communities operating across the many real but traversable geographical boundaries that characterize the Aegean landscape – ridges separating mountain plateaus, rocky coastal stretches between bays, or narrow straits amidst archipelagos. This Element is focused on the less-frequent but impactful long-distance exchanges that connected people in the Aegean with the wider Mediterranean and European world, especially focusing on interactions that may be classified as "economic."

After reviewing definitions and discussing methods and materials available for studying long-distance exchange, the essay presents a diachronic assessment of the geospatial, scalar, and structural characteristics of long-distance exchange and interregional economies, divided into four periods: the Early Bronze Age (EBA), the era of Cretan/Minoan prominence during the Middle Bronze Age (MBA) and Late Bronze Age (LBA), the mature Mycenaean era of the LBA, and the final "Postpalatial" period that closes out the second millennium. A brief concluding section reviews some notable recent developments and persistent interpretative challenges, before closing with a few remarks on the state of the field.

2 Framing Long-Distance Exchange

It is important to understand the history of exchange in the Aegean Bronze Age. Long-distance contacts between the Aegean region, Mesopotamia, and the eastern Mediterranean spurred countless sociopolitical, technological, and economic developments throughout Aegean prehistory. The regular appearance of cultural forms and materials originating to the North in the Balkans and Europe or to the West in the Central Mediterranean likewise cautions scholars against understanding Aegean affairs as regionally insulated. Indeed, a major raft of explanatory approaches in archaeological thought connects major social changes, such as the rise of complex, stratified societies, to matters associated with differential access to rare goods and technological knowledge, such as those secured through exchange relationships. While important, the topic presents a range of challenges, from the conceptual to the empirical, and the field lacks consensus regarding even basic concepts. Arriving at definitional boundaries of scale, context, and structure requires navigating a scholarly environment with widespread disagreement. It is therefore appropriate to begin by establishing working definitions of key terms.

2.1 Exchange: What Is It?

I begin with the notion of exchange. Exchange is a generic term that is analytically elastic, insofar as its basic definition — the act of giving something and receiving another in return – may denote many interactions that do not necessarily fit comfortably under a single heading. Commodity trade, trade in luxury goods, gift exchanges, dowries, symbolic acts of munificence, loans, payments to mercenaries, and many other sorts of exchanges surely populated ancient lives, yet archaeological evidence for exchange is not always conducive to crisp categorization. Exchange, defined as an act, necessarily eludes archaeological sight because actions are not directly visible in the material record. Rather, we possess artifactual proxies from which exchange may be inferred. Most commonly, these take the form of items or technologies that seem to have originated far from where they are observed in the archaeological record. Arriving at the conclusion that such dislocations or relocations were the result of mutual action (giving and receiving) between two willing actors, a meaning implicit in the word exchange, requires inferential and interpretative leaps. Collateral information – such as the existence of technologies probably associated with transactional exchange (e.g., weights) – may provide convincing bases for such interpretations, but they can rarely be truly proven.

That said, since exchange that is economic in nature usually involves physical goods changing hands in a multilateral transaction, it is often more visible in the material record than some other types of exchange. Concomitantly, exchange is often treated as equivalent to the more specific notion of trade in archaeological research. Archaeologists, however, do not operate under a unified definition of trade. I characterize it here as specifically commercial exchange wherein material goods with widely appreciated value are given and received among willing agents pursuing their own or their community's material self-interest (see discussion in Jung 2021). Conceptualizing exchange as trade has the advantage of limiting the analytical framework through which it might be queried. Trade, as opposed to exchange in general, is an explicitly economic concept. Explanatory models about trade can therefore be parsed through the rationalizing logic of formal economic thought. Braudel, for example, found it easy to explain the existence of long-distance trade networks in the sixteenth-century Mediterranean – because they "connect[ed], sometimes with difficulty, regions where goods can be bought cheaply with others where they can be sold for high prices" (Braudel 1972: 442). Along these lines, the logic and purpose of trade lies in its facilitation of profit maximums due to differences in value between source and destination regions. Trade existed, by the same token, for the simple reason that goods were unevenly distributed, and thus had differential values in distinct geospatial contexts.

Viewing trade as an element of the economy is, in sum, advantageous because it makes the expansive toolkit of economic rationality available to the analyst. Yet delving into the realm of archaeological economy comes with its own complications. If exchange is to be efficiently queried through the lens of economy, it is necessary to embed queries in a broader investigation of economic systems. The modern field of economics concerns the production, distribution, and consumption of goods within complex systems made up of manifold actors pursuing material interest through competitive and adaptive engagements with one another. Likewise, scholars of ancient economies focus on the production, circulation, and consumption of goods, as well as the systems or rules (often now conceived of as "institutions") that govern behavior surrounding these processes. Such institutional characteristics may include the organization of labor, the extraction and distribution of resources, the mechanisms of exchange, and issues concerning valuation and demand. Any economy, ancient or modern, is composed of numerous overlapping sectors – for example, the subsistence economy, the industrial economy, or the political economy – all of which interact with and impact one another. Therefore, truly understanding a "trade economy" generally requires its contextualization within a rounded view of the structure, scale, and performance of the economy overall, a view that is nearly always lacking for the Bronze Age.

A question that looms over much discussion of ancient exchange economies concerns whether or not they were capable of facilitating "market" exchange, wherein the value of goods fluctuates due to an automatic "price mechanism" in tandem with fluctuations in supply and demand. While vigorous debate once pitted a modernist/formalist view, according to which ancient economies operated along similar lines as modern market economies, against the primitivist/substantivist view that ancient exchange constituted a primarily social rather than economic endeavor, most now accept a middle path wherein both socially embedded and market-like trade coexisted in most ancient contexts (Bennet & Halstead 2014). Accepting the likelihood of something resembling a market in the Aegean Bronze Age raises the subsequent question of whether Bronze Age economies involved truly "commercial" trade systems, recently defined by Jung (2021: 141–43) as those involving relatively frequent, recurring exchanges of fungible commodities with a generally fixed value produced specifically for the purpose of exchange.

While much evidence sustains a reconstruction of reasonably sophisticated economic trade systems, including something resembling a market with trade in commodities, for some eras within the scope of the Aegean Bronze Age, it is equally apparent that exchanges of different kinds account for as much or more of the evidence. Since prehistoric evidence is often not forthcoming when it comes to clarifying what forms of action might lurk behind the objects in the archaeological record, connecting artifacts that seem to indicate long-distance movements of goods/people to something approximating "the economy" is challenging. Moreover, economic analysis is generally difficult to accomplish for the Bronze Age because the overall complexity of economic systems precludes certain extrapolation from incomplete and ambiguous datasets.

This hazy definitional realm has perhaps contributed to a shift in the language scholars use to describe the movement of objects in the Aegean Bronze Age. The term "connectivity" is now commonly substituted for terms such as trade and exchange in the relevant literature. This term was especially popularized following the publication of Horden and Purcell's influential volume *The Corrupting Sea* (Horden & Purcell 2000). Horden and Purcell saw connectivity as a defining feature of the Mediterranean environment throughout antiquity, yet did not set out a clear definition of this defining feature that could be usefully operationalized in other contexts. Prosaically, we may define connectivity merely as the state of being connected, but the scope of what such a term might mean is (probably purposely) vast. It is not clear how far such a rangy concept might take us analytically. It does prove useful in capturing the extent to which there are many types of "action at a distance" present in the past, and serving as a reminder that sorting among those of an economic nature and those representative of other human processes or motivations must be done with care.

2.2 Modeling Exchange Systems

In circumstances such as the Bronze Age, where the kinds of high-resolution data available for querying modern exchange economies are not available, it is appealing to supplement evidence with theories and models. Archaeologists have rarely used formal or mathematical modeling techniques to query ancient trade systems, but idea-based models have been influential in shaping current discourse about Bronze Age exchange. Such models often position trade within social systems involving status competition, according to which goods functioned as luxury items and markers of high rank (e.g., Voutsaki 2001; Galaty 2018). Models that position trade as primarily motivated by concerns of status competition nest within a wider body of theory known as political economy, a subset of economic analysis that positions political and economic systems and strategies as tightly interwoven elements of a unified whole. Within prehistoric political economies, different categories of exchange have been delineated, including, but not limited to, reciprocal exchange that implicates both political and economic entanglements, redistribution organized to some extent by state actors or bureaucracies, and market exchanges between willing transacting agents (papers in Galaty et al. 2011; Parkinson et al. 2013; Nakassis et al. 2016). Thinking about the political economy encourages consideration of the role of exchange in shaping relations not only within political units (e.g., as a strategy for social differentiation) but also across political boundaries. For example, peer-polity models position exchange as a mechanism for building relationships and jockeying alliances among neighboring communities occupying similar points along a spectrum of developmental political stages (papers in Parkinson & Galaty 2009).

Another influential model has been inspired by the modern concept of World Systems Theory, which – as opposed to the peer-polity model – posits generalizing exchange dynamics that tend to operate between states at different developmental stages, and which are "central" or "peripheral" on a global sociopolitical axis (Parkinson & Galaty 2007; Parkinson 2010). Highly developed core states generally constitute extractive regimes, suctioning up locally unavailable raw materials from peripheral states for deployment in high-level political or economic contexts, while peripheral states are denuded of local resources in exchange for manufactured goods produced in the more advanced core states. Such interactions, in turn, drive increasing economic and political complexity in peripheral states. In the context of the Aegean, the region's position at the periphery of longer-lived and more complex "core" eastern Mediterranean states has led scholars to formulate various models seeking to explain the rise of Aegean states at least in part via their engagement through long-distance trade with Egypt and the Levant (Sherratt & Sherratt 1991; Kardulias 1999).

Also on the scale of the wider Mediterranean stage, observations of the globalized nature of modern economies have encouraged some scholars to posit that certain periods during the Bronze and Iron Ages witnessed similar dynamics (e.g., Sherratt 2003; Choleva 2020: 96–97). Rather than being characterized by clearly distinguishable centers and peripheries, as in a World Systems model, a globalized economy is sufficiently integrated and multimodal that it binds all communities together in ways that affect all relationships, from the global to the local. This obviates efforts to distinguish exchange relationships from one another in kind or systemics because all are thoroughly intertwined through various levels of reinforcement or tension. A globalization model undermines strong distinctions between more and less developed regions and, as such, makes way for postcolonial perspectives on exchange dynamics (Knappett & Nikolakopoulou 2008; Voskos & Knapp 2008). In addition, a globalized approach pushes discourse away from paradigms reliant on monolithic cultural identities and boundaries and encourages the identification of "transcultural" and "hybrid" shared practices that muddy the lines traditional models use to divide up cultures (Stockhammer 2020; Vavouranakis 2020; Knapp 2022). Such ideas emerge in discussions of "glocalism" that have been deployed to good effect in some Bronze Age Aegean contexts (Maran 2011; Galaty 2018).

Studies drawing on formal models have also carved out a space in discourse on Bronze Age exchange. Most prominent among these is network analysis. Networks are made up of relationships, and exchanges comprise an important category of human relationship. Network modeling seeks to clarify the real or theoretical nature, extent, and shape of systems that constitute or govern exchange. Such models may generate a logical basis for explaining why and how certain locations, artifact types, or individuals came to play especially important (or unimportant) roles in mediating, maintaining, or subverting relationships within a system (Knappett 2016). Network science, therefore, has many characteristics that make it appealing as a mechanism for coming to terms with premodern exchange systems (Knappett et al. 2008; Brughmans 2013). In Bronze Age Aegean contexts, formal and informal network-based approaches have been used to generate and test a variety of novel hypotheses about the structure of relational systems (Knappett et al. 2011). In a more general way, this body of research demonstrates the value of collaboration across disciplinary boundaries and the potential for formal, mathematical modeling in a social science tradition that usually relies upon a narrative mode. Other sorts of formal, mathematical modeling apparent in relatively recent scholarship on interaction include spatial modeling (Bevan & Wilson 2013) and agent-based modeling (Chliaoutakis & Chalkiadakis 2020).

Given the tendency to position exchange as a component of economies, it is somewhat curious to observe the dearth of formal economic modeling present in discourse on Bronze Age Aegean exchange systems (cf., papers in Warburton 2022, for a trend in this direction). This gap in part arises from colossal differences between the evidence available for studying modern as opposed to ancient economies, as well as the highly quantitative norms of operation within research on economic history, which confronts archaeological practitioners with very unfamiliar types of discourse, even when the topics discussed have clear comparative value for the distant past. However, there are plenty of areas in economic thought that rely on high-level theories no more quantitatively sophisticated than those encountered in anthropological thought.

A potential path forward in this direction has emerged relatively recently with the application of institutional economic thinking to ancient contexts, although this has developed more strongly as a vector for historical than Bronze Age contexts (but see, e.g., Muhs 2016). Institutional economic thinking concerns the role of institutions, defined as "systems of social factors that conjointly generate a regularity of behavior" and encourage smooth functioning of economic transactions, in determining and shaping economic performance across historical trajectories (Greif 2006: 30). The use of institutional frameworks is by no means a silver bullet for clarifying the history of ancient economies or exchange systems, and a rising chorus of ancient historians has begun to critique these methods (e.g., Bowes 2021; Viglietti 2021). However, there are numerous reasons to posit that centering motivations, strategies, and environments that may have governed transactions in the distant past might be productive in framing prehistoric exchange economies, a point that I return to in the conclusion to this Element.

2.3 Evidence for Exchange

Whatever the model, abstract configurations can only go so far in facilitating evaluation of exchange systems in archaeological perspective. It is generally necessary, at some stage, to also take a close look at the evidence. For archaeologists working in prehistoric contexts, it is most common to rely primarily on the presence and quantity of imported and exported raw materials or finished goods as a proxy for long-distance relationships. The presence of techniques or tools aimed at facilitating production at scales required to fuel export-oriented economies may also be relevant to reconstructing economic exchange systems, as might be the presence of technologies that regulate or mediate exchange. Technologies that make production of crafts more efficient, such as standardization or speed-enhancing mechanisms (e.g., the wheel), might be interpreted as evidence that a community or individual sought to enhance production capacity or speed with an eye to potential exchange markets. The development of standardized weighing systems is usually seen as a strong archaeological indicator that the relevant context witnessed frequent, rule-governed transactions wherein traded goods had fixed, generally agreed-upon valuations. Likewise, seals and sealing practices may indicate the existence of some notional property rights, which tend to arise when regular multilateral exchanges create opportunities to call ownership and its proof into question.

The development of writing systems in the Bronze Age Mediterranean itself may have arisen as a mechanism for facilitating trade and exchange. This observation arises from the fact that many early Bronze Age texts record information about transactions. The earliest such texts belong not to Aegean but to Mesopotamian states, and, in general, the textual record from the Bronze Age is far richer in the eastern Mediterranean than it is in the Aegean. Eastern Mediterranean scribal documents have been fruitfully applied to study of affairs in the Aegean when they are glancingly relevant, but it is not at all evident that fiscal and transactional matters worked the same way in Aegean communities as in eastern Mediterranean ones. The same can be said of later texts in the Greco-Roman tradition that purport to preserve hazy but perhaps vaguely accurate memories of the local distant past. A better resource would be textual records contemporary with and local to the Aegean. Here the record is not particularly rich, because the corpus of extant texts in the only deciphered prehistoric Aegean script, Linear B, is almost completely local in purview, recording economic affairs between state authorities, officials, and other community members. These texts offer some clues to the existence of various types of long-distance exchange relationships but shed essentially no light on the scale, nature, extent, or institutional operation of these relationships. Thus, for the Aegean, the material evidence provides the most robust available basis on which to build up an empirically grounded understanding of exchange.

2.4 Long Distance: What Is It?

To be useful, any discussion of economic exchange must attend to both degree and scale, since trade is likely to have differential impacts on society depending on the frequency, regularity, and quantity of transactions. In the Bronze Age Aegean, exchange probably most often took place at the scale of the "small world," with communities separated by short distances commonly meeting and trading goods regularly, interactions that were undeniably of great importance in shaping society and driving local economic conditions (Tartaron 2013, 2018; Menelaou 2020). My focus here, however, is on long-distance exchange and its impact on the Aegean economy over time.

An important definitional matter, therefore, concerns the distinction between long-distance exchange and other forms of exchange. What counts as "long-distance" as opposed to "short-distance" trade? Observation of existing scholarly discussion supports a general consensus that long-distance exchange is meant to encompass transactions occurring between Aegean communities and communities that were culturally different. Thus, the distinction between regional or local and interregional exchange is seen as analytically and operationally meaningful because it required transactants to engage beyond the boundaries of cultural commonality or political units. This categorical distinction is in accord with tenets of both institutional economics, according to which transactions are more fraught when transactors do not share similar assumptions about cultural norms and morals (Greif 2006), and sociological ideas, such as Bourdieu's concept of the *habitus*, that highlight humans' tendency to experience heightened discomfiture when thrust into unfamiliar circumstances (Bourdieu 1990: 52–65).

A more empirical approach to classifying long-distance exchange might operate according to a standard of actual distance, either conceived in distance-time (e.g., longer than seven days of sailing or walking) or Euclidean distance. Such a definition can, at a minimum, help to clarify and define meaning in scholarly communications. For example, when Papadimitriou states that the distance from Cyprus to the Aegean was "great" in a recent paper, he goes on to explain what he means, rather than leaving the reader to guess (Papadimitriou 2022: 180). The sailing distance from Rhodes (the Aegean island closest to Cyprus) is 220 nautical miles, and Broodbank has calculated an approximate sailing time (in good conditions) of seven to ten hours going east from the Aegean to Cyprus. The reverse trip would have taken considerably longer, due to less favorable currents and winds (Broodbank 2013: 374). No doubt long voyages required specialized infrastructure, knowledge, and tolerance for risk-taking in ways that did not materially apply to shorter ventures.

Yet, a distance measure is not entirely satisfying as the correct gauge for drawing a line between categorically different types of exchange because it elides the real frictions that arise at cultural boundaries and because the technologies involved make this something of a moving goalpost. That shortcoming is especially true in regard to maritime transportation technology and infrastructure. The invention of boats suitable for safely and speedily transporting heavy or bulky goods at a distance would essentially serve to collapse space, transforming what may have been considered "long" voyages into mundane ones. From this point of view, it would be a mistake to see "long-distance" as having a fixed meaning across periods with different maritime technologies.

For example, the boat most often represented in EBA iconography is a longboat that is not clearly suitable for transporting goods on regular long-distance exchange routes (van de Moortel 2017). For an EBA traveler in a longboat, the trip from Melos to Crete might have taken just as long and felt just as risky as a LBA merchant's voyage from Egypt to Crete (Agouridis 1997). Moreover, Broodbank posits that EBA longboats must have been rather difficult and expensive to build. He, therefore, reconstructs both access to boats and participation in long-distance exchange as characteristic of the elite (Broodbank 1989). In this case, trade would likely have been limited to exchange in low bulk luxury items. Third-millennium Aegean communities may have possessed other types of boats better suited to carrying heavy bulky cargo (like metal ores) that do not appear in the iconographical record because they were not associated with elite activities (Jarriel 2021: 124). While it would be optimal to temper a definition of long-distance exchange with detailed knowledge of relative speed and capability of maritime technologies, such information is not always easy to access.

In this context, I adopt a general and flexible definition of long-distance. I focus discussion on exchange that appears to span regional boundaries, requiring travel and transport of more than a few days' time. Most such transactions involved exchange across apparent cultural or political boundaries. My goal is to trace the development and contours of what most scholars in the field seem to identify as meaningfully long-distance and often cross-cultural exchanges. Some variation in the geospatial scope of how this manifests will be apparent, but this is an important point in itself, as the frame of the familiar world likely evolved and flowed over the duration of the Bronze Age in ways amply captured by the evidence for exchange under discussion here.

3 The Early Bronze Age

The Aegean EBA (ca. 3200–2200 BCE) is characterized by the presence of regionally distinct cultures and relatively complex political organizations encompassing the southern Greek mainland, the Cyclades, the Northeast Aegean, and Crete (see Figure 1 for sites mentioned in Section 3). Many of the developments highlighted here are rooted in the second half of the preceding Final Neolithic (FN) period, from the middle of the fourth millennium onward, but limitations of space, and the series' titular concern with the Bronze Age, obviate the possibility of treating their origins properly here.

Although regionalism is a thoroughgoing characteristic of the EBA archaeological record, the period likewise saw the rise of an "international spirit," comprising some shared features and widespread influences (Alberti 2012: 26–27), which likely arose due to supraregional exchange interactions. Such supraregional exchange involved both maritime Mediterranean trade and land-based networks connecting the North Aegean to the Balkans, Anatolia, and points beyond. Interregional trade was facilitated by new technologies, such as seals and weights, that were apparently designed to mediate transactions among parties from different communities. Generally robust and multinodal exchange systems seem to emerge especially during the Early Bronze II period, while the Early Bronze III period was instead characterized by fragmentation.

3.1 Stones

The evidentiary record demonstrates that stones of particular utility were being moved around the Aegean as early as the Paleolithic period. Although it is not always clear whether such movements constituted trade as defined earlier, it is not unreasonable to surmise that, at least occasionally, they did. Among widely distributed stone artifacts from the EBA, chipped stone artifacts suitable for

Figure 1 Map of Aegean sites mentioned in Section 3

cutting, scraping, perforating, and so on form an important category. Metal was rare during the earlier phases of Aegean prehistory, so these stone weapons and tools were used for most tasks requiring a sharp point or blade well into the second millennium. The best quality material available for producing such implements within the Aegean is obsidian, a volcanic glass. There are three sources of obsidian in the Aegean: Melos, Antiparos, and Giali (Renfrew et al. 1965: 229–32). Obsidian exchange networks in the Aegean were focused on Melian obsidian, which has superior utilitarian qualities. Melian obsidian appears to have been the favored material for producing tools from chipped stone throughout Aegean prehistory (Evans & Renfrew 1968; Sampson 1988). By the EBA, it had become widespread, occurring regularly in both habitation and mortuary contexts in the Cyclades (Tsampiri 2018: 37). It also reached north into Macedonia, Thrace, the Ionian Islands, and Anatolia, including sites as far inland as Aphrodisias (Leurquin 1986) and Beycesultan (Lloyd & Mellaart 1962).

There is not a consensus regarding the extent to which Melian communities exploited obsidian resources as a source of wealth or a truly commodified exchange good. According to Mackenzie, the remains of an obsidian workshop for the production of blades to be exchanged on something approximating a market contributed to the prosperity of the community at Phylakopi (Mackenzie 1904: 245). However, Renfrew posited that the quarries were entirely open-access and that anyone sailing to Melos was free to acquire nodules on their own (Renfrew 1972: 442–49). Torrence likewise reconstructed a rather rudderless system, seeing no evidence for specialist resident Melian producers aiming to profit from their own operations (Torrence 1984). This theory perhaps finds support in the existence of local hubs in the south central Aegean that organized the distribution of Melian obsidian from coastal intake points. The lithic assemblages of these sites indicate that they served as locations for the preprocessing of obsidian nodules, with more refined products being then transported inland to neighboring sites (Kardulias & Runnels 1995; Hartenberger & Runnels 2001: 274–77; Karabatsoli 2011: 686–91). Such hubs are especially common in southern Euboea, eastern Attica, and the northern Cyclades.

In addition to obsidian, various types of nonlocal cherts, such as chalcedony and flint, reached Greek sites through northern terrestrial trade routes connecting the Aegean with the Balkans as early as the Paleolithic period. Hard andesitic and rhyolitic stones, especially volcanic andesite from the Saronic Gulf, were harvested and used widely as grinding stones throughout the Neolithic period and the Bronze Age (Bekiaris et al. 2020: 168–70). A substantial deposit of emery (corundite) in northeastern Naxos was exploited and used to generate abrasives conducive to the production of marble and other polished stone artifacts; it is possible that the cultural prosperity of the Small/Lesser Cyclades archipelago in the EBA arose at least to some extent due to the utility of this unusual natural resource (Broodbank 2000: 231–32). Suffice it to say, then, that many types of stone constituted widely valued resources that people would travel long distances to acquire during the EBA. Was trade in stone resources a meaningful part of the EBA exchange economy? Opinions differ about the nature of the voyages by which stone artifacts were procured: were these special-purpose voyages purely aimed at resource acquisition, or might multipurpose trips have integrated short stopovers to harvest material on an ad hoc basis? The consensus is that most stone resources were accessed in a casual, ad hoc fashion like that proposed for Melian obsidian. However, the remains of a possible EBA shipwreck off the island of Dhokos included various stone artifacts, including obsidian tools and andesite grinding stones, finds that may indicate organized, systematic collection and circulation of such resources (Agouridis 1998).

3.2 Metals

Metal ores are unevenly distributed and were highly valued throughout the Aegean Bronze Age. From the date of their earliest exploitation, they seem to have been enmeshed in interregional exchange networks. Copper-, silver-, and lead-bearing ores are abundant among the central-western Cycladic islands and the neighboring region of southeastern Attica. The northern Aegean, especially the island of Thasos and the region of Thrace, also possesses silver and copper ores, as well as rich native gold deposits (Legarra Herrero 2014: 471). Campaigns of material analysis on artifacts from numerous sites have repeatedly indicated that these copper and silver ore sources were widely used in prehistory. The discovery of ample remains of mining and smelting operations in the Cyclades datable to the EBA provides direct archaeological confirmation for at least some of those analytical results (Georgakopoulou 2016: 51–58). Metallurgical ceramics and slags from numerous sites on Thasos likewise indicate that copper production was taking place in the northern Aegean in the third millennium, while fragments of litharge at Limenaria speak to early silver extraction from north Aegean ores as well (Nerantzis & Papadopoulos 2013: 185–92). Gold is consumed in parts of the Aegean, especially Crete, starting in the FN period (Zachos 2010; Legarra Herrero 2014: 468–70, figure 2a–c). Evidence for the use of native Aegean gold sources is elusive since identifying ore sources for gold is chemically difficult, but there are indications that they were exploited starting in the MBA, if not earlier (Pantazis et al. 2003; Rheinholdt 2008).

The systems underlying the production and interregional exchange of EBA metals remain generally obscure. The multimetallic ore deposits at Lavrio in southeastern Attica may have been used as a source of copper ore, but the region's legacy as an aggressively exploited modern mining landscape has annihilated any potential for interrogating its EBA predecessors. Copper-bearing deposits in the Cyclades are smaller in scale than those at Lavrio and have proven less attractive for modern exploitation. As a result, the region's smelting sites are relatively better preserved. Thirteen copper smelting sites and two lead smelting sites have been documented in the Cyclades, and open-air copper mining was likely practiced on Kythnos (Hadjianastasiou 1998; Bassiakos & Philaniotou 2007). The combination of quantitatively formidable slags and a small ore deposit at the site of Skouries on Siphnos indicated to Georgakopoulou that ore was mined from multiple different islands and then transferred to specialized smelting centers, a system that may have prevailed throughout the Cyclades (Georgakopoulou 2016). However, smelting sites are also known from more spatially isolated sites, for example, Chrysokamino and Kefala Petras on Crete (Betancourt 2006) and the Kavos promontory on Keros (Georgakopoulou 2007). The movement of ores to these sites would have required multiple days of travel from the nearest ore sources, hinting at a potentially complex and technologically sophisticated landscape of mining and smelting operations.

In parallel with hypotheses regarding institutions surrounding obsidian exploitation, scholars generally do not reconstruct centralized or controlled governance of access to copper-bearing ores. The larger smelting sites in the Cyclades are not associated with any major settlements. It is possible that control over and access to copper ore resources was not formally governed but rather redounded to individuals or groups who possessed differential access to maritime transportation infrastructure and knowledge of the necessary technological skills (Broodbank 2000: 292–98). These groups probably originated from within the Cycladic region, but it is not impossible that visitors came from beyond the Cyclades to acquire and produce metal (Georgakopoulou 2016: 58–60).

The situation with regard to precious metals and their ores may have been significantly different. Silver production seems to have increased in the Aegean through the course of the EBA. The presence of litharge at numerous sites in Attica, on Siphnos, and on Keros indicates that Lavriotic and Cycladic lead ores were being exploited (Wilson 1999; Georgakopoulou 2007; Kakavogianni et al. 2008; Papadopoulou 2011). This is supported by chemical analysis, insofar as some silver and lead artifacts from EBA contexts in Egypt and the Levant have isotopic signatures consistent with Aegean ores (e.g., Sowada et al. 2023). These developments in the silver production economy occur in tandem with those in neighboring Anatolia, and some silver artifacts in the Aegean come from Anatolian sources, indicating that the two production zones were linked (Gale & Stos-Gale 1981, 2008). Long-distance connections and increasingly complex exchange economies were therefore plausibly connected to demand for silver and silver-bearing ores. This conclusion emerges in part from the observation of a geospatial coincidence between finds associated with silver production and finds related to the emergence of weight metrology as an exchange technology around the same time (Rahmstorf 2015: 165–66).

3.3 Economic Technology

The EBA in the Aegean saw the invention of a local type of standardized balance weight, which was almost certainly instigated by needs associated with long-distance contacts. The primary type of Aegean balance weight is the so-called pestle or spool balance weight. This type was long misinterpreted as a processing tool (hence pestle) or as a decorative item. Early Bronze Age pestles/spools are indeed visually pleasing because they are made from special colorful stones and carefully worked and polished. Rahmstorf finally identified the spool-shaped objects as weights, in part based on the presence of apparent numeric markings on the examples from Tiryns (Rahmstorf 2003: 298–99). Since then, Rahmstorf has catalogued at least 480 examples from seventy-two sites in the EBA Aegean area. The earliest are from ca. 2950–2700 BCE and appear at a small number of sites in the eastern Aegean, for example, Poliochni and Çukuriçi Höyük, where they co-occur with Near Eastern types (Rahmstorf 2016: 256). From 2700 to 2500 BCE, finds of spools/pestles demonstrate a slow spread of weighing technology west toward mainland Greece, where most examples date between 2500 and 2200 BCE. The type dwindles and disappears during the final two centuries of the third millennium.

The weights range from 2 g to 4 kg, with most falling under 100 g. Some are found in sets or concentrations. The existence of accompanying balances is substantiated by pieces or fragments of such at Poliochni, Troy, Küllüoba, Bozhöyük, and Naxos (in the Chora museum). Regions and sites with advanced evidence for silver metallurgy are positively correlated with the presence of spool-shaped balance weights. Rahmstorf argues that weighing practices and the emergence of silver metallurgy occurred in tandem because the two were connected, as traders increasingly needed to ensure equivalencies for valuable materials that came in small quantities. Such a relationship is attested in textual records from the Levant (Rahmstorf 2016: 251). The lightness of the weights certainly supports a situation in which they were primarily used for small transactions in which precious materials were exchanged.

The development of weighing technologies in the Aegean almost certainly occurred due to external influence (Rahmstorf 2016: 257), probably from Anatolia, although Aegean weights are not mere copies of Anatolian ones. Based on analysis of the weights from Çukuriçi Höyük, Cveček argued that multiple variations of transaction technology arose because the intersection of decentralized nonstate societies and an early state society resulted in a low-trust institutional environment that encouraged all transactants to employ their own independent transactional technologies (Cveček 2020). This argument is supported by ethnographic evidence. For example, among the Akan people, both seller and buyer would weigh gold with a separate set of scales, with the seller often using slightly heavier weights in an attempt to generate a higher price (Cveček 2020: 291–92). Bargaining or appealing to a higher authority (a local smith or chief) resolved resulting disagreements. Such a scenario could help to explain why Aegean weights do not simply mimic the shape and styles of Anatolian ones, despite being strongly influenced by Anatolian weights.

Seals and sealing practices provide additional bases on which to reconstruct nascent complexity in exchange systems during the EBA. Early evidence for Aegean sealing practices in the form of clay sealings comes from Cycladic and eastern Aegean islands, at Myrina on Lemnos (Archontidou-Argyri & Kokkinoforou 2004), Zas Cave on Naxos (Zachos & Dousougli 2008: 90–91), Ayia Irini on Kea (Wilson 1999: 166), and

Markiani on Amorgos (Angelopoulou 2006: 221–22). About a dozen sealings have been documented in Early Minoan–Middle Minoan (MM) IA sites on Crete (Rahmstorf 2016: 230). A greater number – in the hundreds – occur in concentrated late Early Helladic II contexts at the mainland sites of Petri (Kostoula 2000), Lerna, and Geraki (Weingarten 2000). The concentration of sealings at just a few sites in the eastern Peloponnese may be a mere accident of the archaeological record (Rahmstorf 2016: 232), or it could signal an advanced episode of economic development (Maran 1998: 432), though the underlying economic basis for such an episode is not immediately obvious. While the sealings from Lerna coincide with other signs of socioeconomic complexity (e.g., the construction of a Corridor House), other sites with Corridor Houses have not produced sealings, while Geraki and Petri have sealings but not Corridor Houses. As with weighing practices, it seems certain that sealing practices in the Aegean were influenced by practices current among communities further east (Maran 1998: 232–40; Maran and Kostoula 2014). This view is supported by strong resemblance between Aegean glyptic imagery and motifs from Anatolian seals (Aruz 2008: 28–29).

Archaeologists interested in the development of exchange institutions in prehistory usually interpret the appearance of technologies for sealing and weighing as a sign of increasing complexity (Rahmstorf 2016: 226). According to this logic, such practices relate to the specific anxieties attendant upon exchange across regional and cultural boundaries in highly valued materials. That line of logic encourages us to consider whether the appearance of seals and sealings at Aegean sites may indicate the involvement of people at those sites in trading precious metals with Anatolian people. This hypothesis gains credence from the shared use and culture of prestigious materials observable across the Aegean, Anatolia, and the Near East, including distinct gold jewelry items such as flat-winged disc beads and quadruple spiral motifs (e.g., Maxwell-Hyslop 1971: 34–37; Aruz 2003; Rahmstorf 2011: 147–49) and semiprecious stones like carnelian and lapis lazuli (Ludvik et al. 2015; Rahmstorf 2015: 162–63). Analysis of gold artifacts from Poliochni, Troy, Ur, and Ebla demonstrates that the jewelry items share not only a common style but also nearly identical chemical compositions, which could mean that all were produced from the same gold source (Numrich et al. 2023). Taken together, the evidence from sealing, weighing, and tastes in precious metal encourage the reconstruction of an extensive long-distance exchange network stretching from the Aegean as far as the Indus valley in the third millennium.

Sealing and weighing are not the only categories of Aegean economic technology whose origins may be connected to external influence. Starting in the Early Bronze II period (2550–2200 BCE), certain communities in the

Aegean begin to fashion pots on the wheel for the first time (Choleva 2020: 64). While not necessarily a purely "economic" technology, the use of the potter's wheel allowed ceramic producers to generate vessels more efficiently (Roux & Courty 1998: 747–48). The adoption of this technology could therefore be connected to emerging economic complexity, whereby producers were concerned to generate enough output to exceed local consumption requirements and therefore facilitate export goods. As with sealing and weighing systems, however, it would be too simplistic to reconstruct the adoption of the wheel in the Aegean as a sign of simple contact followed by "contagious" spread along straightforward lines of mechanical economic logic. For example, wheel-made pottery does not appear on Lemnos, although the site preserves evidence of early influence from Anatolia in sealing and weighing systems. Instead, wheel-made pottery is only present at a limited range of sites within the Lefkandi-Kastri group, located in the Cyclades and southeastern Greek mainland (Day et al. 2009: 335–36). Choleva suggests that these assemblages represent the output of small groups of mobile Anatolian-trained potters who were interested in participating in exchange networks (Choleva 2020: 91–92). Thus, it seems that the use of the wheel was unrelated to efficient or speedy production during the third millennium.

Nonetheless, such technological developments provide a strong basis on which to reconstruct "connectivity" between Anatolia and the Aegean in the Early Bronze II period. There is additional evidence for such connectivity in the form of shared tools for textile production, namely incised biconical spindle whorls and crescent-shaped loom weights (Rahmstorf 2015: 153–56). In the southeastern Aegean islands, cultural affinities and exchanges with Anatolia are sufficiently robust to suggest that these coastal "small worlds" should be perceived as cultural units rather than fissured zones of interaction (Menelaou 2020: 67–69, 2021, 138–41). While the Early Bronze III period is generally a time of significant fragmentation and disruption in those former regions, strong influence from the Balkans' "Cetina culture" becomes apparent in southern Italy, Malta, and parts of the Peloponnese in Early Helladic III, perhaps indicating the rise of long-distance exchange networks in the Adriatic around this time (Maran 1998, 443–50, 2007).

3.4 Ceramic Containers

Imported eastern Mediterranean ceramic containers do not regularly occur at sites in the EBA Aegean (Broodbank 2000: 283–87), though they are present in very limited quantities (e.g., a Syrian bottle at Palamari on Skyros – Parlama 2007, figure 24). Relevant in this regard is the apparent development of the collared jar, invented during this period and used to transport agricultural goods across maritime networks. The collared jar first appears in Early Bronze II, with examples documented from the sites of Poros-Katsambas on Crete, Akrotiri on Thera, and Ayia Irini on Kea (Day &Wilson 2016). Fabric analysis demonstrates that the jars were produced in numerous different locations, including Crete, Melos, Ios, Naxos, Thera, Siphnos, and Kea. On Crete, collared jars do not reach inland sites but remain limited to the coastal production and redistribution center of Poros-Katsambas, near Knossos, which could have served as the main maritime hub for sites in central Crete (Dimopoulou 1997). The overall distribution of these large jars indicates the existence of an "emergent bulk movement of perishable goods in ceramic containers" (Day & Wilson 2016: 21). This might be attributed to an increase in long-distance voyaging, generally increasing complexity of economic institutions, or change in the valuation of agricultural commodities, such as special wines, that generated demand for widespread exchange (Day & Wilson 2016: 31).

3.5 Summary

3.5.1 Geography

By most accounts, Cycladic communities drove what has been called the "emergence of civilization" in the Aegean during the EBA. The strong impact of an EBA Cycladic tradition throughout the Aegean can be seen in material culture, including marble figurines, metal objects, frying pans, long blades of Melian obsidian, and Kampos style pottery. The central actors on the stage of EBA exchange seem likely to have been located in the eastern Aegean and the Cycladic islands as well, with Crete playing an important role, perhaps as an "end consumer" (Legarra Herrero 2014: 483). Crete, Attica, Euboea, and the Anatolian coast demonstrate strong cultural connections with the Cyclades in both material culture and technological knowledge starting in the mid third millennium. Obsidian lithics constituted a major exchange item in the EBA Aegean and traveled impressive distances, given the maritime technology extant at the time. Direct exchange relationships between the Aegean and other regions of the Mediterranean are not strongly evident, but prestige goods show affinities with their Anatolian and eastern Mediterranean counterparts. A considerable evolution in trade networks occurs around the end of Early Bronze II. Closer connections to the North and West are evident in Adriatic Greece, while the Aegean region saw changes that anticipated Crete's centrality to Aegean exchange systems in the MBA (Alberti 2012: 28–30). It is possible that this shift was the result of improved sailing technologies that unshackled Crete from a previous dependence on Cycladic supply lines.

3.5.2 Scale

The EBA is clearly characterized by a great deal of exchange – flows of obsidian and Cycladic material culture outward from the Cyclades and connections between western Anatolian and Aegean groups are apparent across a variety of sites and evidentiary categories, especially artifactual types associated with facilitating trans-actions. Taking into account the sailing technology available at the time, it is not surprising to find that longer-distance maritime flows of objects and ideas direct to the Aegean from distant locations in the central and eastern Mediterranean are limited in scale, or at least visibility. Nonetheless, the emergence of substantial connections in elite exchange networks focused on precious metals and materials is evident. These emergent connections demonstrate a surprisingly close-knit com-munity sharing transactional technologies and exchanging mineral resources ran-ging from the Aegean to Mesopotamia, and even perhaps as far as the Indus valley.

3.5.3 Structure

The picture regarding long-distance exchange in the EBA Aegean is clouded by the generally unforthcoming nature of the evidence. However, it is not unreason-able to reconstruct a scenario wherein the role of direct maritime exchanges among elite groups were decisive factors in shaping interregional interaction (Renfrew 1972; Broodbank 2000). Precocious evidence for growth in sophisti-cated mechanisms for facilitating exchange hints at a connection between such mechanisms and a nascent precious metal exchange network involving silver, produced in Attica and the north Aegean during the EBA. Frangipane's formula-tion of a distinction between wealth systems centered on artisanal and luxury goods and those based on staple goods and commodities provides interesting food for thought in explaining this evidence. In this view, a shift from staple-based wealth to luxury-based wealth in the Near East around the late third millennium BCE correlated with the development of long-distance exchange economies (Frangipane 2018). In a system where wealth is underpinned by staples, wealth cannot be accumulated ad infinitum, because staples are not durable. Thus, wealth in a staple-based system could only be leveraged by constant return to circulation in the form of subsistence provided to a therefore more readily exploitable labor force, or to livestock (Halstead 1981). A transition to a system wherein wealth was accumulated in the form of durable objects made of rare raw materials generated new opportunities for ambitious individuals seeking to accumulate and display prestige and power. In sum, luxury goods are inherently easier to store and share than perishable agricultural goods. They are thus conducive to both new forms of elite practice centered on durable prestige goods and the development of long-distance exchange systems that circulate those goods.

It was previously contended that the Aegean's wealth arose from agricultural abundance in the EBA (e.g., Dickinson 2014: 1867), but this seems increasingly unlikely, especially given the arid climate and limited resources of the Cyclades. The exchange of staples does not seem to have been a core part of the EBA Aegean's involvement in long-distance exchange networks. Rather, interest in rare and unusual metal resources, especially silver, was paramount. Thus, perhaps EBA Cycladic elites pursued strategies of self-aggrandizement through access to rare luxury goods, a pursuit which, in turn, constituted the main aim and structuring force of EBA long-distance exchange.

4 The Period of Minoan Dominance

The MBA is characterized by numerous developments in material culture that coincide with what were apparently transformative changes in Aegean society (see Figures 2 and 3 for the locations of sites mentioned in Section 4). These probably arose in tandem with increasing social complexity and intensification of long-distance maritime contact with eastern Mediterranean communities. At the center of MBA developments lies the island of Crete, which radiated influence outward to the Cyclades and the Greek mainland for much of the period. The MBA on Crete roughly coincides with two architectural phases called the Protopalatial (ca. 1900–1750/1700 BCE) and Neopalatial (ca. 1750/1700–1470/ 1450 BCE). As these names imply, Crete witnessed the appearance of large, specialized complexes, dubbed "Minoan" and "palaces" by their excavators, in two phases. The palatial complexes were probably multifunctional, in part serving as communal gathering centers and spaces for shared ritual events, but perhaps serving as operational centers and domestic spaces for elite ruling groups as well. While certainly derived, in part, from local Cretan antecedents, many characteristics of Minoan palatial society emerged due to external stimulus, especially contact with Egypt.

4.1 Egypt and Minoan Crete

Evidence for the apparently consequential MBA contacts between Crete and Egypt is presaged by more modest evidence for contacts from the EBA. For example, a handful of artifacts from Byblos and Egypt made their way to Crete in the Early Minoan II period (Sørensen 2009: 10–13). Gold is relatively abundant on Crete during both the EBA and the MBA, and there are some compelling reasons to reconstruct Egypt as a source for Cretan gold starting already prior to the transition to the MBA (Legarra Herrero 2011). However, consistent exchange between Egyptian and Minoan elites is only documented starting early in the second millennium (Colburn 2008), when Egyptian stone

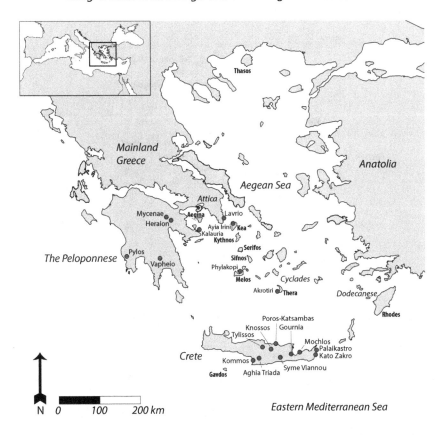

Figure 2 Map of Aegean sites mentioned in Section 4

vessels begin to appear on the island (Watrous 1998; Warren 1969: 71–76, 105–12, 2000; Bevan 2007: 123–25). In Egypt, Middle Kingdom deposits indicate a local taste for Minoan Kamares ware, as evidenced by the consumption of both Cretan imports and local Egyptian imitations (Walberg 1988).

A peak of direct Egypto-Cretan relationships seems to have occurred in the later eighteenth dynasty, during the reign of Thutmose III (ca. 1479–1425 BCE), contemporary with the Neopalatial period on Crete. Egyptian stone vessels began arriving in greater quantities around the transition from the MM III to the Late Minoan (LM) I period (Bevan 2003). The majority came from elite mortuary and domestic deposits excavated at the (apparently politically central) site of Knossos (Murray 2022: 263). There are some indications that a market for stone vessels in Crete arose from increasing status competition among Cretans rather than Egyptian efforts to market their goods. This hypothesis is supported by the fact that Minoan artists sometimes manufactured imitations of Egyptian types and that the Cretan assemblage is dominated by a single type, the

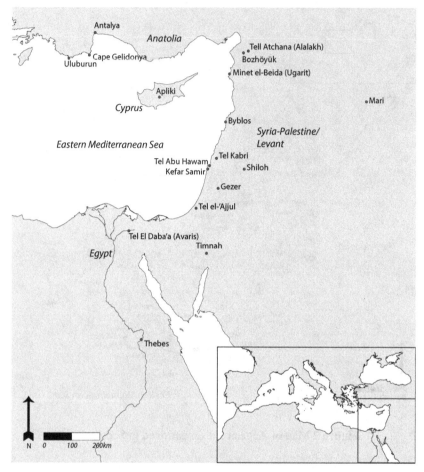

Figure 3 Map of non-Aegean sites mentioned in the text

baggy alabastron made of travertine, which is not likewise dominant in other eastern Mediterranean corpora of stone vessels (Bevan 2007). In the eastern Mediterranean generally, stone vessels likely circulated in high-level diplomatic exchanges with limited relevance to wider swaths of the population, and therefore probably signified elite status (Lilyquist 1996). The Minoan taste for Egyptian stone vessels is probably best relatable back to a broad, if nebulous, sense of elite culture that had a wide valence in many regions.

Additional evidence from beyond Crete supports the reconstruction of a shared multiregional elite culture and reciprocal, perhaps diplomatic, relationships connecting Egypt and Crete in the later MBA and early LBA. The later MBA and early LBA also witnessed the rise of an international style in luxury goods, and techniques associated with their manufacture, evident in similarities between, for example, pendants and jewelry with designs shared between Egypt, Aegean, and Levantine traditions (Kalogeropoulos 2005; Morero & Prévalet 2015). A papyrus from Thutmose III's reign mentions the arrival of ships from the foreign land of Keftiu at the royal docks (Glanville 1931). Representations of people in Cretan dress appear as emissaries bearing gifts in the form of Cretan artifacts in fifteenth-century Theban tomb paintings (Panagiotopoulos 2001). These depictions indicate that recognizable Egyptian luxury products were valued as tokens of long-distance contact. They also demonstrate that Egyptians had a strong sense of who Cretans were and what they looked like (Markowitz & Lacovara 2009).

A related phenomenon is the appearance of wall paintings at Levantine and Egyptian sites that share stylistic and technical characteristics with those executed on Crete (Becker et al. 2018). The relevant sites range from Tell Atchana (Alalakh) and Tel Kabri in the Levant to Tell el-Dab'a (Avaris) in the Nile delta (Niemeier and Niemeier 2000; Morgan 2010). The widespread nature and technical details of this phenomenon have led scholars to posit the presence of traveling Aegean craftspeople throughout the eastern Mediterranean, including in the royal court at Avaris (Cline 1998; Bietak et al. 2007). However, there is a great deal of debate concerning the dating and the proper interpretation of this site; so such conclusions should be handled with caution (Cole 2022).

A brief comment on the Hyksos question is in order since it has implications for the interpretation of some evidence for the chronology and structure of Cretan interactions with the eastern Mediterranean. The Hyksos were non-Egyptian, probably Levantine kings who took control of Egypt during the fifteenth dynasty (ca. 1630–1530 BCE) as the result of an apparent military invasion. The site of Avaris was the Hyksos capital, and thus some interpret the evidence for Aegean-style frescoes at Avaris as a token of diplomatic or commercial exchange between the Hyksos interlopers and Cretan authorities. Against the interpretation of a Hyksos–Avaris–Crete connection is the bigger picture, in which Aegean influence or style in Egypt seems filtered mainly through Levantine agents, rather than direct interaction with Egypt. While there are numerous Hyksos artifacts from Cretan deposits, the consensus seems to be that these most arrived in Crete subsequent to the Hyksos period, as exchanges between the Aegean and Egypt appear to have resurged during the eighteenth dynasty. For example, a travertine lid inscribed with the name of Khyan, a Hyksos king, was recovered from a mixed layer at Knossos that also contained LM IIIA material, which would date the sealing of the deposit well after the end of Khyan's reign around 1600 BCE (Phillips 2008: 97–98). Given the Levantine origins of the Hyksos, one possibility is that Hyksos artifacts arrived in the Levant during the Egyptian Second Intermediate Period and then later made their way to the Aegean through Levantine–Aegean exchange networks that intensified during the LBA (Cole 2022: 258–59). This conclusion is also supported by Barrett's study of MM ceramic imports in Egypt, which appear to cease during the Hyksos interregnum (Barrett 2009).

4.2 Minoan Long-Distance Exchange beyond Egypt

Robust exchange relationships between Minoan Crete and other parts of the Mediterranean are not overwhelmingly evident, but there are indications that the Minoan sphere of exchange did extend to the Levant, Cyprus, and Anatolia. This is entirely logical because the physical constraints of long-distance travel in the MBA and LBA Mediterranean made maritime exchange systems generally conducive to multiregion engagement (Papadimitriou 2022: 179). Any ship heading to Crete from Egypt would have had to pass through ports in the Levant, Cyprus, and Anatolia as a matter of maritime necessity (Sauvage 2012: 273–88).

Neopalatial exchange relationships between Crete and non-Egyptian communities are demonstrated by data from both within and beyond the island. A small amount of Minoan pottery has been recovered from MM–LM I deposits in the Levant, mainly at Byblos and Ugarit (Minet el-Beida), and the pseudo-*koine* in fresco style and technique discussed earlier extended to the Levantine sites of Tel Kabri and Alalakh, where a few Minoan artifacts have also been documented (Sørensen 2009: 18–20). The distribution of Minoan material in the Levant is primarily coastal, although a few items come from sites further inland along the Orontes and Jordan Rivers, perhaps representing the material residues of inland Levantine trade routes. Levantine imports in Crete from these periods are likewise scarce, precluding a reconstruction of the nature or structure of any Levantine–Minoan contacts at the MBA to LBA transition based purely on imported prestige goods.

More informative are data regarding imported raw materials and technologies, especially those concerning metallurgy. A tin ingot was discovered in an apparently ritual sixteenth-century deposit from the site of Mochlos in central Crete (Berger et al. 2019). Tin deposits are not present in the Aegean; so this artifact is sure to have arrived on the island from elsewhere. Isotopic analysis indicates that the tin likely originated in central Asia, which accords with roughly contemporary Akkadian sources identifying tin sources in the same region (Foster 2016: 115). Copper ingots dating to the Neopalatial (LM IB) period have been discovered at several palatial sites (Stos-Gale 2011: 223, table 22.1; Kassianidou 2014). According to isotopic analysis of the lead contained in the ingots, they seem to come from at least two different sources. The isotopic signature of the ingots from Mochlos, Gournia, and Syme Viannou is consistent with Cypriot ores, while that of ingots excavated at Aghia Triada and Tylissos points to a non-Mediterranean source. Isotope data from the Kato Zakros ingots is not consistent. Some are consistent with Cypriot ores, while others are consistent with non-Mediterranean ores (Gale 2011: 218; Stos-Gale 2011: 222–26). At the coastal sites of Palaikastro, Poros-Katsambas, and Kommos, the presence of tubular bellow pipes for enhancing the output of copper smelting blast furnaces, a technology first developed on Cyprus, in MM III–LM I contexts indicates that the technologies associated with metalworking were also brought to Crete by long-distance exchange partners (Papadimitriou 2022: 182). This evidence is tantalizingly lacunose but certainly creates an impression of widespread contacts between Crete and multiple exchange partners outside of the Aegean.

Texts from the archives of Mari, located in modern Syria, reinforce the archaeological picture of long-lasting and purposeful exchange between Crete and the Near East beyond Egypt during the early and middle second millennium. These texts mention numerous possessions from Kaptara, a term thought to indicate Crete, potentially as early as the nineteenth century and definitely encompassing the eighteenth century, during the reigns of Yahdun-Lim and his son Zimri-Lin (Malamat 1998: 34–35). The Cretan possessions recorded in the nineteenth-century texts include shoes and gold bowls, while the Zimri-Lin archives mention Cretan shoes, belts, textiles, weapons, metal vessels, a Minoan boat replica, and a mace decorated with lapis lazuli (Sørensen 2009: 14–15). The latter item offers a glimpse of complex, multistage exchange dynamics since the lapis lazuli would have originally reached Crete as a traded raw material, and then returned to the east as part of a multimedia manufactured product (Colburn 2008: 208). Finally, the description of Zimri-Lin's trip to Ugarit records the proffering of a modest quantity of tin, perhaps between 650 g and 5 kg, to two Cretans, who may have constituted either a royal delegation or some sort of trading contingent at the Levantine port (Guichard 2005: 162–68). The presence of an interpreter with the Cretan visitors adds weight to the notion that such interactions were regular enough to have generated such specialized roles necessary for smooth communication between culturally diverse trading partners (Helzer 1989: 12–13).

The existence of a wide and complex pan-Mediterranean exchange system during the Neopalatial period can be further appreciated from finds at Crete's own apparent port or harbor sites. It appears that metals arriving on the island may have been received and processed at Poros-Katsambas, a site on the Trypeti hill northeast of modern Heraklion that was probably associated with or politically subordinated to the palatial center of Knossos. Already demonstrating strong connections to the Cyclades in the form of imported pottery and obsidian from its foundation in the EBA, the site has produced evidence for metal, pottery, and perhaps faience production from the Neopalatial period (MM IIIA–LM IA). Indications of long-distance trade connections are present in the form of Egyptian scarabs, a Levantine seal, and a Canaanite jar, as well as raw materials, such as ingots (Dimopoulou 1997; Serpetsidaki 2012: 166–67).

Kommos, located on the long sandy coast of the Mesara region in south central Crete, provides additional evidence for Neopalatial coastal communities' engagement with long-distance exchange routes. Imported pottery is present from the MM IB period and continues to appear until the end of the LM IIIB period, after which the site is abandoned. In the LM III period, considerable investment was made in the construction of a large, galleried building facing the sea that has been persuasively interpreted as a shipshed (Shaw & Blackman 2020). Protopalatial imports at Kommos mainly comprise other Aegean material (e.g., from the Cyclades, elsewhere on Crete, and Gavdos), but by the LM I period, Cypriot tableware is present alongside Canaanite jars, Egyptian amphorae, and one western Anatolian amphora (Rutter 2006: 651–56).

It is interesting to observe the presence of non-Aegean transport vessels at Kommos, given the absence of such material at contemporary inland Cretan sites. Such a contrast might provide a basis on which to reconstruct Kommos' role as that of a depot for ships heading along a coast-hugging trans-Mediterranean voyage rather than as a primary destination well-integrated into the local economy. A similar situation might be reconstructed for the eastern Aegean island of Rhodes, which lies on a crucial maritime route and probably had independent and strong connections with Cyprus throughout the MBA and LBA (Karageorghis & Marketou 2006; Marketou 2014).

4.3 The Wider Aegean Situation

Cycladic sites of MBA and early LBA dates are not particularly well-documented, due to a combination of modern overbuilding and a limited legacy of archaeological excavation. Sites like Ayia Irini on Kea, Akrotiri on Thera, and Phylakopi on Melos indicate that dense, sometimes fortified, coastal towns may have constituted the main settlement type; large palatial complexes of the type that developed on Crete are not present. At the same time, influence from Crete is evident starting in the early LBA, including Minoan architectural forms and the introduction of some technologies (Knappett & Nikolakopoulou 2008; Nikolakopoulou & Knappett 2016). Extra-Aegean exchange networks may have connected Cycladic communities with the wider Mediterranean, but a situation in which Cretan agents handled or mediated most long-distance exchange relationships, with imported objects and ideas filtering through to Cycladic sites as a result of Cretan influence rather than independent contacts, has seemed more likely to some scholars (discussion in Nikolakopoulou 2009).

This view, and the generally related concept of "Minoanization," is not universally accepted and is certainly not the only way to interpret the archaeo-logical data (Knappett & Nikolakopoulou 2008; Gorogianni et al. 2016). The site of Akrotiri on Thera provides a case in point. Starting in the late MBA, Akrotiri's material culture demonstrates significant cultural influence from Crete. At the same time, Akrotiri's LB I assemblages also include imported objects from other Cycladic and Aegean islands, Crete, the Greek mainland, Cyprus, Egypt, and the Levant, and locally produced artifacts demonstrate knowledge of manufacturing techniques that originated elsewhere (Dawson & Nikolakopoulou 2020). Likewise, the presence of balance weights indicates that agents on Thera understood the standardized value systems of the period and could have participated in independent market exchanges absent Cretan inter-vention (Michailidou 1990).

Indeed, based on models of the contemporary Aegean maritime network, Knappett et al. (2011) argue that Thera was a crucial hub for Minoan exchange, such that its elimination subsequently caused a slow decline in trade, ultimately disrupting distributional systems sufficiently to precipitate the breakdown of economic and sociopolitical systems overall (cf., Driessen & Macdonald 1997; Driessen 2019). Such an argument, if accepted, would highlight the intertwined and interdependent quality of Neopalatial exchange systems. While Crete may have operated as a center of gravity for long-distance and diplomatic exchanges with, for example, Egypt, perhaps nodes of particular connectivity were ultimately more decisive in shaping the flow of material exchange and communication.

The archaeological evidence is not particularly forthcoming when it comes to the question of what Aegean communities were offering to exchange partners. Cretan artifacts have been found on Cycladic islands, at sites in coastal Anatolia, and in the Dodecanese, but Aegean exports in the eastern Mediterranean remain scarce (Merrillees 2003; Papadimitriou 2012: 97–99, 114; Karageorghis et al. 2014). Aegean pulses are known from sites on the Carmel coast in the Levant (Kislev et al. 1993; Mahler-Slasky & Kislev 2010), but this does not provide sufficient evidence for reconstructing regular staple exports. One possibility is that archaeo-logically invisible materials, such as textiles or purple dye, were paramount among Minoan exports. Alternatively, Papadimitriou has made the novel suggestion that Cretans offered the technology of writing to Cyprus in exchange for copper (Papadimitriou 2022: 184).

Another possibility is that the presence of sites along the "Western String" of Cycladic islands (Siphnos, Serifos, Kythnos, and Kea) reflects an economic interest in extracting silver from Attica for exchange in long-distance trade networks (Sherratt 1993; Davis & Gorogianni 2008: 345). The presence of MBA/LBA smelting bellows at Thorikos and nearby Ayia Irini on Kea may be related to the processing of Lavriotic metal resources (Papadimitriou 2020: 175–76). Silver is scarce at MBA sites in the Levant, but hoards appear along the southern Levantine coast, at sites such as Gezer, Shiloh, and Tell el'Ajjul, beginning in the MB III and MB–LB transitional periods. However, an outgoing silver trade from Lavrio during the Neopalatial period is not supported by recent analysis of these Levantine silver hoards. Rather, the hoards appear to include northern Aegean silver resources from the island of Thasos (Eshel et al. 2023: 10).

In general, there is scant evidence for strong connections between the Greek mainland and distant regions during the MBA and early LBA, though the island of Aegina was probably an important producer of export-oriented pottery within Aegean exchange networks (Alberti 2012: 33). Only a handful of sites on the mainland, two in the Argolid (the Argive Heraion and Mycenae), two in the southern Peloponnese (Pylos and Vapheio), and one on the island of Poros (Kalaureia), have turned up any Egyptian imports prior to the Late Helladic (LH) II period. It is often assumed that the mainland had little to no direct contact with the east during this period, but rather accessed imports through Cretan contacts, a position that is substantiated by the presence of Cretan luxury products at the same mainland sites that produced imports (Murray 2022: 262–63). Evidence for later MBA and early LBA Mainland Greek connections with other regions, especially to the north, is treated in Section 5.

4.4 Summary

4.4.1 Geography

Crete was likely the most important hub for Aegean long-distance exchange. Other regions of the Aegean may have been less engaged with the broader Mediterranean, unless via interactions that were mediated through Crete. This seems certainly true of the mainland but less so for the Cyclades and southeastern Aegean islands, which retained strong links with one another and other regions, including Anatolia and Cyprus. It is apparent that different scenarios should be envisioned for exchange across material categories. Items valued among an international elite for prestige value, perhaps including stone vessels and Kamares ware, circulated in small numbers, while it is possible that Aegean silver was extracted and exchanged through some other means or networks, perhaps governed or mediated to some extent by Cycladic communities.

4.4.2 Scale

While robust communication among a small group of artisans and elites must be reconstructed by way of explanation for the stylistic *koine* emergent in some media during the Minoan Palatial period, it is difficult to substantiate a quantitatively large amount of material exchange moving in and out of the Aegean at this time. Aegean ceramics in Egypt and the Levant are scattered and idiosyncratic, while eastern finds in the Aegean are neither varied nor numerous. It is possible that archaeologically invisible materials, such as textiles, or materials that have not yet been extensively subjected to chemical analysis to determine their source, such as silver, were circulating in quantities not apparent in the extant evidence. Altogether, on current view, it seems the scale of long-distance exchange was limited, although its cultural impact looms large.

4.4.3 Structure

Diplomatic and artistic contacts may be reconstructed among Cretan, Egyptian, and Levantine elite communities during the Protopalatial and Neopalatial periods. The consensus seems to be that interactions between Cretan and Levantine or Egyptian people probably involved royal gift exchanges, the movement of artisans, or intermarriage, as opposed to commercially driven motivations (Sherratt 1994: 238; Cline 1998: 209; Laffineur 1998: 67; Sørensen 2009: 24). At the same time, the existence of a commercial market involving exchange of silver and copper resources, perhaps with Akrotiri serving as a hub, finds support in the archaeological data from a few coastal sites and in some extant metallurgical and isotopic data.

5 The Mycenaean Aegean

The later prehistory of the Greek mainland is usually divided into the Early and Late Mycenaean periods (see Figure 4 for a map of Aegean sites mentioned in Section 5). The Early Mycenaean period begins around 1600 BCE (the transition from the Middle Helladic [MH] to LH ceramic phases) and is characterized by the appearance of richly furnished tombs that were probably related to increasing political complexity, perhaps including the appearance of nascent chiefly states. The Late Mycenaean period, beginning around 1400 BCE (LH II/LH III transition), signals the maturation and extension of these chiefly states. Late Mycenaean states (or according to some, "the" Mycenaean state) developed shared hierarchical political structures with a king, called a wanax, at their apices. The wanax resided in a specialized architectural complex that we refer to as a palace, with attributes that are not unrelated to but in some ways distinct from the complexes referred to by the same name on Minoan Crete. The archaeological remains of several palatial sites include accidentally burnt administrative texts, known as Linear B tablets, that provide information about fiscal concerns of the palatial bureaucracy. Several material cultural indicators suggest that Late Mycenaean polities exercised region-wide authority in some parts of Greece. Although the issue remains much debated, it is also apparent that Mycenaean states eventually overtook Minoan ones as the dominant cultural and political force within the Aegean.

The transition to the LBA in the Aegean is thus characterized by major geopolitical and socioeconomic changes. It also ushers in a new phase of exchange from a variety of perspectives. The first is geospatial. With the

Figure 4 Map of Aegean sites mentioned in Section 5

appearance of Shaft Graves bulging with exotic luxuries at mainland sites and the rise of Mycenaean states, the mainland takes on a newly central role in the story of Aegean long-distance exchange. The second is scalar. The quantity of artifactual evidence for exchange between Mycenaean and distant communities implies an explosion of trade during the fifteenth and fourteenth centuries, at least compared to what had come before. The third is typological. All available evidence points to a period of commerce in fungible goods, wherein exchanges focused as much on raw materials and resources as on luxury finished products. The fourth is granularity and detail of evidence. Because of the kind and quantity of evidence available for the LBA, we are on relatively firm footing when it comes to making confident statements about the details of exchange relationships.

5.1 Shipwrecks and the Geopolitics of the Late Bronze Age Mediterranean

It is reasonable to begin with the latter point because the LBA shipwrecks that have been discovered in the Mediterranean are both spectacular and extraordinary sources of information for the topic at hand (Bass 1991). The crown jewel of these is no doubt the Uluburun shipwreck (Pulak 2008; for other wrecks, see, e.g., Phelps et al. 1999; Spondylis 2012; Bass & Hirschfeld 2013; Öniz 2019). The ship went down sometime near the end of the fourteenth century in the Gulf of Antalya, near the modern seaside town of Kaş. Considerable debate surrounds its likely origin point and destination. Based on the combination of eastern Mediterranean commodities and Aegean artifacts considered "personal items" (stirrup jars, a flask, razors, swords, etc.) in its cargo, many scholars consider it likely that the ship originated somewhere in the Levant, perhaps Ugarit, and was destined for an Aegean palatial site (Pulak 2008: 301–02). Charming corroboration for the Levantine origin of the ship is provided by the skeletal remains of a stowaway mouse (Cucchi 2008). Prominent among its cargo were bulk goods, including 10 tons of copper ingots in various shapes, 1 ton of tin ingots, 170 glass ingots, hippopotamus teeth, elephant tusks, and approximately 150 Canaanite jars full of valuable commodities, such as resin or resinated wine, plus a bit of gold and silver scrap (Pulak 2008: 293–95).

The fascinating remains of the Uluburun wreck sparked immense interest in the role of long-distance trade in the LBA Aegean. They provide, therefore, a fitting jumping-off point for a general discussion of the geopolitical and institutional parameters of trade in the LBA. The question of why such a ship should be heading to the Greek mainland in the fourteenth century is a good place to begin. As discussed earlier, mainland polities were likely not as intensively involved with long-distance Mediterranean exchange networks as Cretan ones during the first half of the second millennium. It is clear that Crete was instrumental in the emergence of complex palace-centered states on the mainland. Cretan influence on the mainland was probably initially mediated through communities on the islands of Kythera and Aegina, where signs of sociopolitical complexity and mercantile initiative precede the appearance of mainland Shaft Graves. For example, Aeginetan islanders exported distinctive, volcanic-tempered pottery throughout the Aegean (Gauß et al. 2015), and a spectacular burial containing a gold diadem, bronze weapons, a boar's tusk helmet, and imported pottery from Crete and the Cyclades likely reflects wealth accruing to a local merchant elite from trade in the MH III period (Kilian-Dirlmeier 1997).

Beginning around the transition from the MBA to the LBA, a few mainland communities appear to connect with lucrative exchange routes extending north and west, probably at least in part motivated by the desire for materials like gold and amber. The rise of a mercantile elite on the mainland is most evident from finds in Shaft Graves from the Early Mycenaean period (ca. MH/MM III–LH/LM I). Mycenaean Shaft Graves contain gold, silver, amber, bronze, and other precious materials in impressive quantities. For example, the Shaft Graves at the site of Mycenae contained thousands of luxury objects, including gold and silver jewelry, sheet gold ornament in many shapes and sizes, gold plating, amber beads, crystal scepters, ostrich egg, stone, and faience vessels, inlaid wooden boxes, metal vessels in copper, silver, and gold, and over 100 swords and daggers, many with gold inlay. The gold contents alone weigh almost 15 kg (Stos-Gale 2014: 185).

Many of the high-value goods in mainland Shaft Graves are Cretan imports or demonstrate substantial Cretan influence and craftsmanship. However, other finds indicate that the sudden wealth of the mainland elite arose from the opportunistic exploitation of long-distance contacts independent of Crete. The quantity of amber finds – 1,290 pieces of amber were deposited in Mycenae's Shaft Grave IV in Grave Circle B – points to a Baltic or European source for the gold, and some of the silver is chemically consistent with a Carpathian origin (Stos-Gale 2014: 199). The distributional patterns of Egyptian and Mesopotamian beads in the Balkans and Europe provide further indication that the Aegean might have carved out a profitable role as a middleman in trade between northern regions and the eastern Mediterranean (Varberg et al. 2016). Isotopic analysis has shown that two women buried with a large amount of wealth in the Shaft Graves at Mycenae were not born in the Aegean, and it is plausible that they arrived at Mycenae through an elite marriage alliance with trade partners (Nafplioti 2009). Overall, we can reconstruct a situation in which Peloponnesian communities grew increasingly wealthy based on their strategic location on trade routes that formed a nexus between Minoan Crete, the eastern Mediterranean, and the Baltic and Transylvanian regions beginning around the transition from the MBA to the LBA (Graziadio 1998: 29). This wealth gave rise to increasingly evident sociopolitical hierarchy and complexity.

Notwithstanding the rise of mainland elites, Cretan long-distance connections with Egypt and the Levant stretch onward into the LBA. A papyrus from the reign of Amenhotep II (1427–1401 BCE) describes ships from Keftiu (Gundacker 2017); the London Medical Papyrus, from the eighteenth dynasty, includes spells written in the Keftiu language (Quack 2022: 57, 88–89, 101, 137, 154); and an inscription on the base of a colossal statue of Amenhotep III (ca. 1390–1350 BCE) at Kom el-Hetan (Thebes) lists the toponyms of both Knossos and Mycenae (Cline & Stannish 2011). Ugaritic texts from the thirteenth century place the god Kothar-wa-Khasis, who presided over art, crafts, architecture, and engineering, as a Cretan resident (Sørensen 2009: 33, table 3, nos. 1–4), perhaps representing a memory of the Minoan era and a recognition of the technical virtuosity of Cretan arts. Cretan individuals and shipments are also listed in LBA administrative texts from Ugarit (Sørensen 2009: 24).

At the same time, moving forward into the final phases of the Bronze Age, the cultural and political roles of Crete and the mainland seem to reverse somewhat, to the extent that a strong scholarly consensus positing a military takeover of Crete by the Mycenaeans has long stood, despite recent protests and debates (e.g., papers in D'Agata et al. 2022). In any case, the importance of mainland communities as partners in long-distance exchange relationships with extra-Aegean communities during the period of the mature Mycenaean state seems certain. By the later fourteenth and thirteenth centuries, the quantity of eastern Mediterranean imports on the Aegean mainland is much greater than the quantity at Cretan sites outside of the likely transshipping port of Kommos (Murray 2017: 84–85). Finds from Mycenaean palatial contexts in central and southern Greece include a range of *exotica*, including finished luxury or ritual items, ingots, transport vessels (especially Canaanite jars) that probably held agricultural or craft products (Rutter 2014; Day et al. 2020), and luxury items generated locally from imported exotic materials such as ivory and lapis lazuli (Tournavitou 1995; Burns 2012). Metal artifacts are concentrated around palatial sites, a distribution that may reflect efforts by palatial elites to monopolize or restrict access in order to enhance their own social and political standing (see data compiled in Kayafa 1999).

In general, however, the assemblage of imported objects in Late Mycenaean sites does not support a scenario in which the only form of trade operated at a high diplomatic level controlled by elite agents. The imports present at each individual palatial site are variable in terms of their material characteristics and likely points of origin, which provides some basis upon which to reconstruct rather rich and complex extra-Aegean contacts for Mycenaean palatial sites (Murray 2017: 76–85). Finds from the LM III A–B periods at Kommos likewise support the existence of a wide and complex pan-Mediterranean exchange system that operated – at least in some contexts – at the independent behest of traders and merchants. The LM IIIA2–LM IIIB periods saw a peak of imports, both in terms of quantity and quality of material, at Kommos. Canaanite Jars, Cypriot storage containers (pithoi) and tableware, Egyptian and western Anatolian amphorae, and Sardinian bowls and jars attest to the continuing role of the harbor as a stopover or depot for ships plying a route between the Levant and Sardinia, even as the quantity of imports on Crete overall declined in the same period (Rutter 2006; Day et al. 2011). Additional exogenous material from the site includes bronze ingots and scrap as well as gold, amethyst, and lapis lazuli jewelry (Dabney 1996: 263–64). The strong contrast between the archaeological record at Kommos, with ample evidence for multidirectional long-distance contacts, and the finds from other LM IIIA2–IIIB sites on Crete, which preserve few exotica from beyond the Aegean, makes plausible the notion that this port served as an independent mercantile operation during the later phases of the LM III period.

This observation invites us to revisit a prominent question surrounding the Uluburun wreck: the institutional context and agency behind its dispatch. Does the wreck and its cargo exemplify state-sponsored trade, private trade, gift exchange, or a noncommercial transaction of a different nature? Given the massive, and massively expensive, specialized cargo, it is often presumed that the ship was dispatched through state agency with a particular destination in mind, rather than constituting a more diffuse and opportunistic tramping mission. Monroe calculates the financial loss represented by the ship's demise as approximately 12,000 silver shekels, or the equivalent of yearly wages for 1,000 workers (Monroe 2020: 26–27). The scale of this investment might support the interpretation that the shipment was financed by a state. However, it is not impossible that wealthy merchants of the sort documented among the great houses of Ugarit could have underwritten such a vast cargo. Thus, the sheer scale of the wreck cannot prove the nature of its institutional background with certainty.

A common interpretative strategy relies on equating the Uluburun cargo with the quantitatively impressive diplomatic exchanges recorded in the Amarna texts, a corpus of royal correspondence between the Egyptian Pharaoh and other kings of eastern Mediterranean states of the LBA recovered from archives at the Egyptian royal site of Amarna (Moran 2002). A compelling counterpoint to this strategy made by Zangani is that such analogies ignore the complete absence of Aegean entities in the Amarna letters (Zangani 2016). This absence could arise from random gaps in the archival record rather than serving as evidence that Aegeans never engaged in reciprocal diplomatic exchanges with eastern Mediterranean states. However, that is certainly a plausible explanation of the evidence, and Zangani presents a compelling case for positioning the Uluburun shipwreck as the disastrous outcome of a different category of exchange between the Aegean and eastern Mediterranean states. While the diplomatic royal exchanges described in the Amarna letters appear to be mainly rhetorical and symbolic in nature, Zangani argues that most Mycenaean engagement with the eastern Mediterranean was primarily commercial.

Whether one accepts Zangani's argument or not, it is a welcome reminder that it would be a mistake to categorize all LBA Aegean exchange relationships under any heading or category. The distinctive repertoire of Mycenaean ceramic exports in different regions around the Mediterranean likely also speaks to the variable institutional relationships between the Aegean and various trading partners. Mycenaean exports in Egypt, for example, are nearly all closed vessels, are relatively widely distributed, and are rarely marked with Cypro-Minoan symbols, which is distinct from the situation on Cyprus and the northern Levant (Hirschfeld 2004; Bell 2006: 59). Finds from Mycenae indicate that there may have been a special diplomatic relationship between its *wanax* and the court of Amenhotep III (Cline 1995; Phillips & Cline 2005; cf., Phillips 2007).

Thus, a direct trade relationship may be posited between the Aegean and Egypt. On the other hand, the more limited distribution of Mycenaean vessels (i.e., to a few sites in the kingdom of Ugarit and the site of Alalakh; see Koehl 2005) and the better-documented (if still minor) presence of Cypro-Minoan potmarks in northern Syria (Hirschfeld 2000, 167–68) have led some to posit that Mycenae interacted indirectly, through Cypriot middlemen, with that region (e.g., Papadimitriou 2022: 187).

That Cypriot merchants served as intermediaries for Mycenaean long-distance trade is suggested, if not made certain, by several lines of circumstantial evidence: the presence of Cypro-Minoan marks on Aegean pottery from various locations within and outside the Aegean (Hirschfeld 2004), general Cypriot marking practices in Mycenaean contexts (Donnelly 2022), Cypriot drinking and eating vessels and practices at Aegean harbor sites (e.g., Tomlinson et al. 2010; Rutter 2012; Karageorghis et al. 2014, 32–33, 220–27; 267–69, 277; Sienkiewicz 2022), re-carving practices apparent on the cache of lapis lazuli cylinder seals from Thebes (Smith 2022), and ethnic indicators referring to possible Cypriots (*ku-pi-ri-jo, a-ra-si-jo*) in Linear B texts (Shelmerdine 1998: 296; Bennet & Halstead 2014). Taken together, available evidence alerts us to the variety of dynamics likely governing long-distance exchange institutions in the Aegean LBA. Some exchanges may have constituted elite diplomatic interaction between political entities, while others were conducted through mercantile mechanisms, either directly or via intermediaries.

5.2 Commodity Exchange

As this complex scenario would seem to demand, the world of goods crisscrossing the Mediterranean in the LBA was expansive. Luxury goods and diplomatic gifts likely continued to circulate among elites, as they had since the EBA. Alongside this venerable tradition of exchange in luxury goods among the elite, new – or at least newly perceptible – systems and standards supporting more trade in raw materials developed. Transactional technologies serve as one index of these developments. Weights and weighing practices are widely evident and evidently advanced during the LBA (Alberti et al. 2006; Ialongo & Rahmstorf 2019; Ialongo 2022). Likewise, institutional technologies like writing, sealing, and the establishment of legal frameworks (plus the means for their enforcement) develop in all of the kinds of ways we would expect in an environment where cross-cultural transactions among self-interested parties were becoming more frequent, perhaps even somewhat regular features of economic life.

Bronze was an important LBA commodity and was probably often exchanged in such transactions. Several standardized formats of copper and tin ingots were developed in the later phases of the Bronze Age, presumably in order to facilitate the exchange and transportation of these important resources. The most important of these were bun and oxhide ingots, the latter category being most visible in LBA deposits. It is also likely that copper circulated in scrap form (Gestoso-Singer 2015). While copper ingots on Minoan Crete likely arrived from a variety of locations around the Mediterranean, as already discussed, nearly all such ingots subjected to analysis indicate a source on Cyprus from around 1400 BCE onward. Especially important, and perhaps used exclusively after about 1250 BCE, was copper from the Apliki region of the Troodos mountains (Stos-Gale et al. 1997; Gale 2011: 214–15).

Among other archaeological indicators of the mercantile nature of Cypriot LBA society (Knapp & Meyer 2023), this evidence has led to a widespread appreciation of Cypriots' role in the LBA metals economy. Cyprus possesses ample copper resources and preserves excellent contexts that shed light on the attention paid to copper extraction and processing on the island (Charalambous & Webb 2020). Isotopic analysis of artifacts, however, does not support the reconstruction of a monolithic source of Aegean copper in the Mycenaean period. Instead, such analysis identifies Sardinian and local Aegean sources as prominent alongside or instead of Cypriot ores, depending on the site (Kayafa 1999). Some concerns about the accuracy of inferences based on lead isotope analysis have been voiced, but it seems straightforward enough to conclude that multiple copper sources were often used in the LBA, while at the same time recognizing that Cypriot mercantile initiative prominently shaped circulation and consumption patterns (Knapp 2011: 250–51).

Aside from the Uluburun tin cargo, few tin ingots are known from LBA contexts, and none postdating the Mochlos ingot have been encountered in Aegean contexts. Tin ingots from the thirteenth and twelfth centuries that have been recovered in Israeli contexts are consistent with an origin distinct from that of the Mochlos ingot, most likely somewhere in northern Europe, Iberia, or Cornwall (Berger et al. 2019), and perhaps arriving on the same trade conduits as the amber that becomes apparent in the archaeological record around the same time (Woudhuizen 2017: 342). The tin from the Uluburun wreck is not consistent with those sources but most likely originated in Egypt, India, or Sardinia (Powell et al. 2022). These results preclude simple conclusions about the supply of tin to the Aegean in the LBA, but the large number of bronze objects in Aegean deposits of the fourteenth and thirteenth centuries provides assurance that supplies were arriving in quantity.

Another raw material that circulated in Mediterranean LBA trade networks was glass, primarily from Egyptian and Mesopotamian sources. About 200 glass ingots, weighing 460 kg, were present onboard the Uluburun shipwreck, along with 30 relief beads in Mycenaean style that are logically most likely to have been possessions of the people aboard the ship, rather than cargo intended for exchange. Both the ingots and the relief beads were produced in Egypt, but chemical and compositional analysis indicates that they came from different workshops, the beads from around Amarna and the ingots from elsewhere (Lankton et al. 2022). It appears that many beads recovered from contexts within the Mycenaean Aegean came from the same manufactory center as the Uluburun ingots, which should lead us to expect that different ships carrying similar cargo, at least where glass is concerned, arrived in the Aegean prior to and following the disastrous voyage of the Uluburun. Glass, frit, and faience objects, especially beads, are regularly found in impressive quantities at LBA Aegean sites. Some of these materials were manufactured in the Aegean using raw plant ash (Nikita & Henderson 2006; Nikita et al. 2009), but many other finished beads were imported through exchange networks, as was the technology for glass production (Polikreti et al. 2011).

Among ceramic imports to the Aegean, Cypriot tablewares and pithoi are present in modest quantities at LBA sites. Stockhammer has convincingly argued that such quantities are depressed by the difficulty of recognizing ceramic imports when extant as fragmentary sherds; so this quantitative evidence should not be taken as an indication of the modest role of Cypriot pottery in long-distance exchange systems (Stockhammer 2015: 178–79). Canaanite jars, meanwhile, have been identified at numerous sites in the Aegean including Kommos, Pylos, Tiryns, and Mycenae (Rutter 2014; Day et al. 2020). These jars could have carried a variety of commodities, including terebinth resin, resinated wine, glass beads, lamps, and so on, that had bulk value (Jung 2021). However, the appearance of some jars in mortuary contexts may belie a simple interpretation of mobile vessels as mere containers.

What kinds of products might people in the Aegean have been providing in return for shipments of goods like copper, tin, glass, and ivory in the Mycenaean Bronze Age? A major change in the long-distance exchange scenario during the LH III period as compared with previous periods concerns exports from the Aegean to the eastern Mediterranean. While the quantity of tablewares that apparently made their way from Crete to Cyprus, the Levant, and Egypt during the Minoan palatial periods was modest, at least 7,000 LH IIIA2–B vessels of Mycenaean manufacture have been identified at numerous sites in these regions (Steel 2013: 130–31; Zuckerman et al. 2020). Additional exports reached the coast of Anatolia to the east and Italy to the west, with the latter group coming from distinctive production centers in western Greece (Murray 2017: 191, table 4.4; Matricardi et al. 2021). In other words, Aegean finewares genuinely explode onto the Mediterranean scene starting in the LH IIIA2 period. The pace of export saw an apparent decline in the middle of the LH IIIB period, perhaps presaging the evolution of LBA exchange systems apparent in the succeeding LH IIIC period, as discussed in section 6.

Many exported Mycenaean vessels were probably valued for their own aesthetic appearance or exotic cachet. For example, pictorial style kraters seem to have been made in the northeast Peloponnese specifically for export to Cyprus and the Levant, where they are prominent in elite mortuary contexts (Sherratt 1999: 187–88; Steel 2004). The production of Mycenaean-style pottery outside of the Aegean among communities that apparently had an appetite for such decorated wares also indicates its independent valuation as a desirable good (Bettelli 2022). In general, though, most Mycenaean pottery exports are containers rather than tablewares, and it is very likely that the stirrup jars and flasks that make up a majority of the exports contained liquids, especially perfumed oil. Perfumed oils probably made up a sizable portion of exported Mycenaean goods (Fappas 2012), a conclusion that is based on both the archaeological evidence and numerous Linear B texts that record major unguent boiling operations (Palaima 2014), though such unguents could have been used to treat textiles in addition to serving as export goods (Shelmerdine 1995: 103). Analysis has shown that most Mycenaean fineware vessels from the eastern Mediterranean were manufactured in the Argolid (e.g., Mommsen et al. 1992; Mountjoy & Mommsen 2001, 2015), perhaps with oil imported in coarse transport stirrup jars from central and western Crete (Haskell et al. 2011). This evidence sustains the reconstruction of a rather sophisticated vertically integrated system of production, transportation, and packaging for the Mycenaean unguent manufacturing industry.

Crete was more than a mere supplier of raw materials within complex chains of production and distribution to suit palatial mainland purposes. At least some sites appear to have engaged independently with long-distance exchange routes throughout the LBA. This is true of Kommos but also evident elsewhere. A case in point is the site of Kydonia (modern Chania). Although only partially excavated due to its position underneath the modern town, ample evidence, especially an impressive quantity of Cypriot imports, demonstrates its role as a hub for trade (Andreadaki-Vlazaki 2015: 28; Hallager 2017: 47–49). Of equal importance is the wide distribution of pottery from a distinct regional Kydonian workshop, which stretches from Sardinia to the west, throughout the Greek mainland and the Cyclades, and east to Cyprus, the Levant, and Egypt (Hallager 2017: 47–49).

Other sites on Crete, such as Mochlos and Petras, received imported pottery from eastern Aegean islands such as Kos (Morrison et al. 2022), indicating that localized exchange networks were exploited in different parts of the island in ways likely outside the purview of Mycenaean or palatial oversight. This view is supported from evidence in the Dodecanese. Although there is no clear palatial presence in the region, sites on Rhodes and Kos always possessed strong connections with Anatolian and eastern Mediterranean communities (Girella 2005: 132–36; Vitale & Trecarichi 2015), indicating the existence of operational and probably mercantile exchange systems that may have been distinct from those discernible from mainland palatial evidence.

Aside from pottery and its contents, could the Mycenaeans have offered other materials or finished goods to their exchange partners? Other possible exports from the Aegean to the eastern Mediterranean include silver and textiles. It is possible that silver was the primary commodity that bound the Aegean into Mediterranean trade networks from the EBA onward (Sherratt 1993). However, considerable doubt remains about the extent to which Aegean states extracted and marketed Lavriotic silver on LBA exchange markets (e.g., Wood et al. 2021). Complicating matters is the emergence of some indications that silver diminished in importance in the LBA following its nascent use as a currency in the later MBA (Eshel et al. 2023). Linear B records from Knossos indicate that Mycenaean polities produced many textiles, and it is not implausible that colorful woven cloth constituted another important Aegean export (Nosch 2014).

5.3 Summary

5.3.1 Geography

During the latter phases of the LBA, Mycenaean long-distance exchanges connected the Greek mainland to the wider Mediterranean in seemingly robust and explicitly commercial ways. All evidence points to a situation in which the palatial state or states of the central and southern Aegean were the leading consumers and producers of goods for lucrative and well-developed central and eastern Mediterranean exchange markets in the fourteenth and thirteenth centuries. That said, routes crossing the Aegean brought long-distance exchange goods to ports outside of this core region, a reality that is particularly evident at coastal sites that lay along such routes, such as Kommos on Crete and Ialysos on Rhodes.

5.3.2 Scale

The quantity of evidence for exchange in the Late Mycenaean period is greater than what came before, but this should not necessarily be taken as evidence for a thick, dense array of exchange relationships in the LBA. It has been posited that the quantity of material moving around through long-distance trade routes was never substantial enough to have a major impact on societies or political economies at any point in the Aegean Bronze Age, including the LBA (e.g., Snodgrass 1991; Cherry 2009). Conversely, other scholars have positioned regular, robust long-distance exchange relationships as a strong force operating on local dynamics (see discussion in Tartaron 2013: 23–27). While this debate was never explicitly resolved within Aegean scholarship, it seems that many scholars espousing "connectivity" as a driving force in Mediterranean prehistory must implicitly accept that exchange and trade had an immense and far-reaching impact during the LBA (e.g., Broodbank 2013; Galaty 2018). This is not entirely consistent with efforts to come to terms with the true quantitative scale of available evidence (Parkinson 2010; Murray 2017), nor with recent efforts to turn analytical attention away from long-distance exchange dynamics towards more frequent and probably denser local "small-world" networks (Tartaron 2013; Pullen 2023). Thus, the question of scale in the LBA exchange economy remains something of a muddle, at least in my view.

5.3.3 Structure

The LBA preserves robust evidence for the emergence of markets for relatively regular commodity exchange in the kinds of fungible goods characteristic of mature economic systems, in addition to the evidence for exchange in luxury goods apparent in preceding periods. Mycenaean LBA communities were engaged in commodity manufacturing that was specifically intended to facilitate entry into exchange markets. It is plausible to reconstruct the existence of an LBA Mediterranean exchange market in fungible goods that probably coexisted and partly overlapped with elite, symbolic, and diplomatic exchanges. A strong vein of evidence indicates that merchants, intermediaries, and harbor or port personnel played a role within this economic market that was, at least in part, independent of strong state control. Cypriot mercantilism was important throughout this period in the form of copper production and marketing, and perhaps more broadly as facilitating middlemen for some interregional trade.

6 The Postpalatial Period

A complicated set of apparent crises beset the eastern Mediterranean around 1200 BCE, famously precipitating the demise of many of the complex states that had grown up around its shores in the preceding centuries (Knapp & Manning 2016). In the Aegean, palatial sites suffered episodes of destruction, and distinctive material–cultural hallmarks of palatial assemblages fall out of production in the LH IIIC period (ca. 1200–1050 BCE). An increase in wealth, and perhaps political independence, is apparent in other regions and sites (especially coastal regions and sites) that were not characterized by palatial architecture, a phenomenon that has been interpreted as the result of changing political landscapes (e.g., Knodell 2021, 120–22). Overall, then, the story of society following the demise of palatial states is uneven, with completely different scenarios emerging from the evidentiary record from region to region and even from site to site (see Figure 5 for location of Aegean sites mentioned in Section 6).

6.1 Structure and Agency in Postpalatial Exchange Economies

As discussed in the previous section, long-distance exchange has been seen as a central driving force behind the rise of complex states in the LBA eastern Mediterranean. It is apparent that the mature Mycenaean states cultivated and maintained long-distance exchange ties. Accepting this generates an expectation that the dissolution of states would likewise be intertwined in some causal direction with long-distance exchange operations. If elites in Mycenaean states leveraged differential access to special, exotic goods from abroad in order to

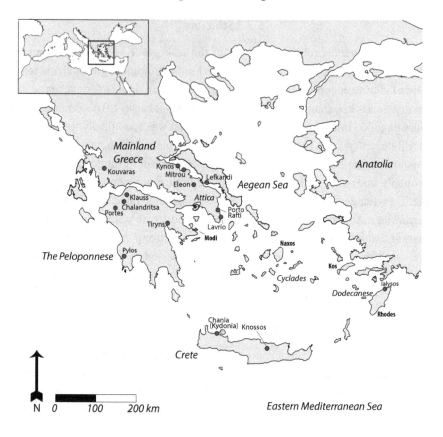

Figure 5 Map of Aegean sites mentioned in Section 6

reify their status at the top of the sociopolitical hierarchy, disruptions to the supply of such goods could have proved disastrous to the rulers' ideology, and ended in their demise. From another point of view, if palatial states served as either the main consumers or administrators of long-distance exchange, such that their absence left a vacuum in either the demand for exotic goods or the institutional structures and personnel that had organized supply of such goods, we might expect to see a steep decline, or even a complete cessation, in extra-Aegean exchange following ca. 1200 BCE.

Various implicit or explicit formulations of such scenarios can be glimpsed widely in academic discussions of LH IIIC long-distance exchange. However, such views are no longer particularly prevalent. In part, this is because the evidence increasingly demonstrates that there was not such a steep decline in exchange during the Postpalatial period as was once accepted. Equally import-ant have been arguments to the effect that merchants and traders were as influential as states in driving and administrating exchange during the palatial

LBA. This latter swell of argumentation encourages some modification to Sherratt and Sherratt's influential transitional model, according to which state-sponsored and often diplomatic LBA palatial exchange gave way to private, merchant-driven, commercial trade at the transition to the Iron Age (Sherratt & Sherratt 1991). Many scholars would probably now question the strength of such a contrast, insofar as merchants and markets independent of state control have come to figure more prominently in discussions of LBA trade (Monroe 2009; Knapp 2018; Pullen 2021).

Overall, it is more accurate to describe the long-distance exchange environment of the twelfth century as yet another evolutionary phase than as a period of exceptional disruption. Comparison between the raw number of imports identified from LH IIIC sites shows an overall decrease in comparison to those from LH IIIB sites, but I have argued that this is probably related to a decline in the overall population as opposed to a decrease in the intensity (on a per capita basis) of exchange relationships (Murray 2017). A compelling question concerns the mechanisms that facilitated such exchange relationships, as many artifactual indicators of transactional technologies, like weights and sealings, largely disappear along with the states that likely issued some of them in the LBA (Murray 2020). Evidently independent merchants found a way to adapt and trade without the help of such tools, because there is plenty of support for a continuation of interregional interaction and exchange following the palatial period.

Some sites, like Tiryns (Maran 2004; Vetters 2011; Stockhammer 2008, 153–61; Maran & Papadimitriou 2021), Knossos (Coldstream & Catling 1996: 194–95), and Kydonia (Hallager & Hallager 2000) and strategically positioned islands, like Rhodes, apparently retained the strong long-distance connections they already possessed in the fourteenth and thirteenth centuries (Benzi 2013; Zervaki 2022). Other areas of the Aegean that do not seem to have been particularly well-integrated into the long-distance exchange economy in the thirteenth century show new evidence of connections in the twelfth. This is true of the mountainous western Peloponnesian regions of Elis and Achaea as well as the central Greek sites of Kynos, Mitrou, Lefkandi, and Eleon (Knodell 2021: 124–25), the Cycladic island of Naxos (Vlachopoulos 2012: 295, 298; Vlachopoulos & Georgiadis 2015), the bay of Porto Rafti in Attica (Murray et al. 2022), and even such improbable locations as the jagged islet of Modi, which lies just off the east coast of Poros in the Saronic Gulf (Konsolaki-Yannopoulou 2019). Recent analysis of a distinctive pottery fabric called White Ware, probably manufactured in the bay of Porto Rafti, shows a wide-ranging distributional pattern that speaks eloquently of the extent to which relatively long-distance exchanges of pottery remained robust in the

LH IIIC Aegean, although along different geospatial lines than the routes reconstructed for the palatial period (Lis et al. 2020, 2023).

6.2 A Possible Bronze Shortage

What other changes can be detected in the evidence for twelfth century exchange economies? Here it is germane to return the spotlight to shipwreck archaeology. While the cargo of most metal-bearing LBA shipwrecks contained at least some "fresh" material in the form of raw ingots, a ship that wrecked along the coast of Anatolia near Cape Gelidonya, at the end of the modern Tekke peninsula west of Antalya, was carrying a load of mainly fragmentary metal objects, probably best interpreted as scrap metal. The date of the shipwreck, around 1200 BCE, and the perception of collapsing Postpalatial trade routes, has led to much discussion about the possible roles of recycling, reuse, and scrap metal circulation (Bass & Hirschfeld 2013; Gestoso-Singer 2015), the increased importance of independent merchants, and a notional bronze shortage in the Postpalatial period.

Some have found independent verification of a bronze shortage in the small quantities of bronze distributed to smiths at the Mycenaean palace of Pylos immediately prior to its destruction (Blackwell 2018), and a longstanding hypothesis attributes the adoption of iron in the Aegean Early Iron Age to such a shortage (Snodgrass 1971: 246–49). On the other hand, bronze artifacts remain rather common, and are indeed widely distributed, in Postpalatial Aegean deposits (Murray 2017: 168–72). Rather than showing radical change, chemical analyses of the bronze from the Gelidonya wreck are consistent with the scenario for the fourteenth and thirteenth centuries, with most copper in the ingots apparently coming from Cyprus and copper in finished artifacts sourced to Aegean and Anatolian sources (Lehner et al. 2020: 163). The possibility of a copper shortage is made improbable by the strong relationship apparently retained between the Aegean and Cyprus in the twelfth century. Mycenaean pottery, and imitations of Mycenaean pottery produced on Cyprus, becomes so abundant on the island that many have posited sizeable out-migration from the Aegean to Cyprus (Mountjoy 2018). But it takes more than copper to make bronze, and the question of tin sources following the geopolitical disruptions of the final Bronze Age remains open. It is possible that a decline in tin supply led to metallurgical crises in the Postpalatial Mediterranean, but recent evidence for varied tin sources in the Bronze Age Mediterranean overall may suggest that such supply lines were more flexible than was previously appreciated (Berger et al. 2019).

Despite apparent continuity in Aegean–Cypriot relations during the twelfth century, substantial dynamism in the copper ore economy is apparent beginning in the eleventh century. While it is still detectable (e.g., in a cist tomb at Kouvaras in Aitolo-Akarnania, Stavropoulou-Gatsi et al. 2012), the prominence of Cypriot copper in the Aegean declines after the eleventh century. Meanwhile, copper from desert deposits in southern Sinai and Jordan, which occurs in some twelfth-century ingots, becomes widely exploited during the eleventh to ninth centuries (Yahalom-Mack et al., 2014: 173–74; Kiderlen et al. 2016; Ben-Dor Evian et al. 2021). This might indicate that change in systems of metal supply was a factor shaping Postpalatial exchange relationships.

6.3 West and East in Postpalatial Long-Distance Exchange

Several lines of evidence indicate newly strong connections between the Aegean and the Adriatic in the Postpalatial period. In the twelfth century, the quantity of Mycenaean style finewares and other elements of Mycenaean material culture increased at numerous sites through Sicily and South Italy. Analysis of glass objects from Postpalatial funerary assemblages shows that these were now arriving to the Aegean from the Adriatic region (Nikita et al. 2009). At the same time, artifacts (especially bronzes) and practices with pedigrees from the north and west become a part of typical Aegean mortuary repertoires, especially in the western Peloponnesian regions of Achaea and Elis, which demonstrate a surge in wealth around this time (Giannopoulos 2008), but also in other regions like the Argolid (Van den Berg 2018) and the eastern Aegean (Zervaki 2022). Bronze Italic-style artifacts from northwestern Peloponnesian sites like Chalandritsa, Klauss, and Portes seem to have been manufactured locally in the Aegean from Cypriot copper (Jung et al. 2008; Aktypi 2017). Among these artifacts are many examples of a type of sword, called the Naue II sword, that seems to have brought its users an advantage in combat (Jung & Mehofer 2013: 178–83). Various hypotheses surround the seemingly new forces binding together the Adriatic, the Aegean, and the eastern Mediterranean in the latest phases of the Mycenaean period, whether trade alliances or a different sort of relationship involving, e.g., military engagement (Jung 2009; Jung & Mehofer 2009, 2013).

A compelling line of interpretation especially put forward by excavators at Tiryns, but also likely applicable to other assemblages, posits that the evidence of nonlocal forms of practice, including craft production, should be taken as an indication of the widespread presence of people with nonlocal cultural affiliations instead of simply serving as an indicator of trade relationships (Maran 2004; Stockhammer 2008, 153–61; Kostoula & Maran 2012; Vetters & Weilhartner 2017). Additional evidence for mixed communities may include a striking increase of variability in mortuary ritual and grave types (Girella 2005: 136–38; Palaiologou 2013; Zervaki 2022). While indicators for such mixed communities continue to accumulate, a scenario in which the Aegean was home to cosmopolitan communities with a range of strong connections stretching from Italy and Sardinia to the west, through western and Central Crete, encompassing the northwestern mainland, and passing through northern and eastern Aegean routes towards Anatolia and Cyprus, is just beginning to come into focus.

6.4 Summary

6.4.1 Geography

The exchange networks of the Postpalatial Aegean trace distinct paths, from Italy in the west to Rhodes and Cyprus in the east, and through the Euboean gulf to the north Aegean. Disruptions in the Levant and Egypt perhaps truncated the eastern extent of these networks, but the western and Central Mediterranean became newly important exchange targets for the Aegean in the twelfth century, in ways that may be seen as foreshadowing the strong links between the Aegean and southern Italy that would become such a characteristic of historical Greek political geography (Papadopoulos 2001; Blake 2014). The demeanor of Aegean settlement in this period seems strongly maritime in character, with almost all well-connected communities nestled, frog like, up against the shores of the Aegean. In some cases, this was taken to the extreme, with apparently mercantile communities occupying tiny islets like Modi in the Saronic Gulf and Raftis in Porto Rafti bay.

6.4.2 Scale

It is difficult to gain clarity on the scale of exchange in the Postpalatial period, but the old view that trade routes and long-distance networks essentially fell silent after the palatial collapses can no longer be easily sustained. As more attention has been devoted to LH IIIC material, it has become increasingly evident that many communities remained engaged in long-distance relationships of various kinds in the new institutional environment of the twelfth and eleventh centuries. The example of White Ware demonstrates a range of distribution evocative of the palatial period, while new metal types and technologies seem to have been circulating from the Balkans to Italy and throughout the Aegean region.

6.4.3 Structure

While it remains likewise difficult to discern a clear structure or set of aims in a Postpalatial long-distance exchange economy that is only just starting to come into view, some initial observations may be put forward. First, there is a maritime focus to both settlement and exchange networks, and little evidence for flows of goods or commodities from coastal sites inward to hinterland regions through local mechanisms. This is likely attributable to the generally weak terrestrial political institutions characteristic of the Aegean during the twelfth century, which might have served to facilitate redistribution of goods acquired through maritime exchange to inland centers. Second, cosmopolitan mercantile communities engaged in craft production and exploiting legacy exchange contacts that may have been initially cultivated through state-oriented networks can be posited as the main agents supporting exchange systems and interregional economies. In an institutionally poor environment, it is likely that personal relationships and shared goals recognized among merchants provided the main structuring forces governing exchange during this period.

7 Changing Currents and Future Directions in Aegean Trade and Economy

As has no doubt become clear by this point, the topic of long-distance exchange and interregional economies in the Bronze Age Aegean is a rich one. The field is likewise constantly evolving, as a dense and devoted network of scholars regularly produce new empirical, theoretical, and methodological advances that keep progress moving forward. In this final section, I provide a few general comments on new developments and potential paths forward in this area of research.

7.1 New Discoveries and Techniques: Shipwrecks, Ore Sources, Lignite, and Beyond

An exciting and challenging aspect of archaeology as a discipline is that new discoveries continuously require practitioners to reevaluate and recalibrate interpretations and overall narratives. The pace of underwater discoveries has quickened in recent decades, in part due to increasingly sophisticated remote sensing and recovery techniques, and this has obvious implications for the study of long-distance exchange networks (e.g., Spondylis 2012; Öniz 2019; Agouridis & Michalis 2021; Hadjidaki-Marder 2021). Likewise, new analytical technologies are beginning to crack nuts that long seemed impenetrable, such as identifying ore sources for tin, silver, and gold (Berger et al. 2019; Powell et al. 2022; Numrich et al. 2023). Along the same lines, new techniques allow archaeologists to investigate hitherto entirely unimaginable lines of questioning. A striking example of this comes in the form of dental analysis proving individuals at the citadel of Tiryns in the Argolid inhaled bucketloads of smoke from the combustion of lignite that must have been carted to the site across the mountains of Arkadia (Buckley et al. 2021). If the technological advances and intensifying efforts of recent decades give any indication of what is to come, it is likely that answers to many questions we have not even conceived of asking may be coming down the research pipeline sooner than we might think.

7.2 Categorizing and Interpreting Proxies for Exchange and Mobility in a Cosmopolitan World

Sometimes, however, the introduction of new techniques and lines of questioning create a muddle where we once thought we had clarity. In the realm of long-distance exchange, recent interventions increasingly indicate that people and things in the Bronze Age moved around in quite a lot of ways that are difficult to distinguish from exchange, as defined here, and splicing apart these different types of movement can be quite challenging.

The potential material cultural impacts of interregional exogamy were already mentioned briefly in connection with the phenomenon of Aegean-style wall paintings in Tell el-Dab'a and regarding two wealthy women among the individuals interred in Mycenae's Shaft Grave burials. These are but two examples of evidentiary cases in which it is reasonable to surmise that exogamy might account for the mobility of women – and their possessions or attendants – in the LBA (Gorogianni et al. 2015; Cutler 2019). Another category of individual that may have been rather mobile in the Bronze Age was the skilled craftsperson. As early as the eighteenth century, a communique among merchants at the Old Assyrian site of Alishar documents a fuller being sent across the territory as a loan (Dercksen 2001: 43–44, 62). Attestation that specialized workers were treated as a kind of exchange good in the LBA is abundant in the corpus of the Amarna letters (Zaccagnini 1983: 249–50), and other texts indicate that such mobile workers could have been seized as slaves or captives as opposed to serving as gifts or trade "goods" among state agents (Michailidou & Voutsa 2005: 26–27). Blackwell has made a convincing case that stoneworkers and builders in the Aegean either learned directly from or included workers from Hattuša, the capital of the Hittite Empire (Blackwell 2014). The Mycenaean Linear B tablets from Pylos record females with ethnonyms that refer to locations in the eastern Aegean, such as Miletus and Lemnos (Shelmerdine 1998: 295; Olsen 2014: 95–100) and to "Asia," plausibly interpreted as a reference to the Levant (Michailidou & Voutsa 2005). Many scholars have posited that potters were mobile in various guises throughout the Bronze Age (e.g., Abell 2014; Lis 2018). If these lines of evidence and argumentation may be relied upon, they present a Mediterranean Bronze Age environment wherein weavers, masons, sculptors, and carpenters were often at work in locales far from their original homes. Additional evidence points towards a potential population of mobile military personnel in the LBA (Schofield and Parkinson 1994; Abbas 2017; Jung 2018; Kelder 2022).

In such an environment, it can be difficult to be sure that the evidence we might interpret as a suitable proxy from which to discern long-distance exchange really pertains to that topic. Instead, objects may have arrived in regions outside of their area of manufacture because they belonged to these kinds of mobile individuals. Such observations lead us to two important points. The first is that the watery Mediterranean was a rather fluid place during the Bronze Age, with people and things moving around in equal measure and for a variety of reasons. The second is that untangling which archaeological evidence for extra-Aegean exchanges pertains to what kind of movement remains a formidable interpretative challenge.

7.3 Institutions and Bronze Age Long-Distance Exchange Economies

In providing some consideration of how one might drill down from a nebulous world of connectivity and interaction to studies that hone sharply in on the realm of exchange in its formal sense, I return briefly to the topic of institutional economic thinking raised in the introductory section of this Element. While exchange can take many forms and is not particularly well-theorized or standardized in its manifestation within archaeological literature, the specific act of transacting is the subject of immense and thorough discourse in the literature of institutional economics. Co-opting this body of discourse might assist prehistorians hoping to invigorate discussion of the economic logic and agency that lurks behind the static objects that we interpret as mobile within the archaeological record.

As noted earlier, institutional economics generally center the transaction, and the social and institutional armature that grows up around the acts that make up exchange systems. Thinking about such armatures along institutional lines can provide elegant explanations for the basic features of an economic system. For example, the institutions of fixed pricing and standardized weight metrology are not merely conveniences in a technical sense. Rather, they provide a combination of empirical solutions and regular social practices that reduce transaction costs by limiting information asymmetries between the customer and the seller, thus enhancing confidence on both sides of an exchange act. An interesting observation about ancient weights in general is that they are not particularly standardized (Schon 2015; Ialongo & Rahmstorf 2019), and this observation can be extended to supposedly standardized types of transport container (Kotsonas 2014). Such variety within standardization raises the possibility that the function of weighing and other superficially standard practices was more closely related to generating regularity of behavior and a sociology of assurance around risky or frightening transactions rather than to genuinely ensure fair and balanced trades in a way that is consistent with Northian institutional economic thought.

Like any framework, institutional economic thinking has merits and drawbacks. However, there are several reasons we might expect that ideas from institutional economics can be helpful for studying Bronze Age exchange systems. The first is that, although the act of transaction is invisible to archaeologists, much of the evidence available from which to reconstruct Bronze Age exchange systems concerns transactions – this includes much of the lacunose textual data, but also the extensive metrological remains. The second is that institutional economics has a strongly historical element, in that it is very concerned to explain how and why institutions change over time (North 2005). Something that emerges from the preceding review is that Bronze Age exchange systems show considerable diachronic dynamism. Thus, we have a powerful intellectual remit to explain how and why such changes occurred, and why exchange economies took different forms in different technological, geopolitical, and social environments. Thinking through static systems, as we now know, has not been conducive to generating such explanations; perhaps institutional thinking may offer richer, or at least original, possibilities.

A third merit of institutional thinking is that it encourages comparison and interdisciplinary communication. Discussion of the LBA Aegean economy is frequently elided from conversations about the historical trajectory of economic developments in Greek history. Perceptible is a longstanding disinclination among Greek historians to take seriously the Bronze Age economy as relevant or interesting to the bigger picture of Aegean economic developments. This situation is not ideal, because it hinders interdisciplinary comparative analysis, which can be generally powerful in opening up new interpretative pathways not available in an intellectually insular environment. It is also deleterious because it shackles us within the flawed assumption that prehistoric people were fundamentally simpler or less entrepreneurial than modern ones and blinkers any view of how insights from the Bronze Age might impact questions of general humanistic and social scientific interest when it comes to economic systems. Perhaps describing the Bronze Age economy in terms of institutions could be generative of powerful new explanatory models while also further eroding longstanding and counterproductive disciplinary fissures.

8 Conclusions

Whatever the future holds, discussion of long-distance exchange and interregional economies will surely retain its position as a robust and constantly evolving subfield of Aegean prehistory. Systems of exchange arising from both internal dynamics within and influences from beyond the Aegean were important in shaping historical and cultural evolution throughout the entire Bronze Age. These systems often pertained to economic developments, but their impacts also seem to have reverberated in politics and culture. While the raw realities of resource distribution and the cachet that inherently accrued to artifacts and materials that were locally scarce sometimes resound as the major factors shaping the structure and social purpose of long-distance exchange, far more complex aspects of interaction, hybridity, and cultural mixing are often perceptible in the evidence as well.

The geography of long-distance exchange shows interesting variation over time. The island-centered and perhaps egalitarian systems of EBA resource extraction and distribution give way to the Crete–Egyptian diplomatic and artistic exchanges of the Minoan period during the MBA, perhaps due to technological factors that changed the reality of maritime travel. During the LBA, mainland interaction with the Balkans, Europe, and the Central Mediterranean opened up new realms of material exchange possibilities, ultimately embedding the Aegean in a vast pan-European/Mediterranean Bronze Age world system with a mature commodities trade and many institutional players that probably included both merchants and states in equal measure. The final phase of the Bronze Age saw the demise of many state operators, but independent traders and merchants survived to reshape the landscape of exchange and interaction to suit the new environment, which returns in some ways to the highly maritime and rather unregulated scenario observable in the EBA but with an expanded geospatial range. The overview presented here brushes up against many equally important issues that far exceed the scope of what is possible in a relatively brief synthetic treatment, including but not limited to political landscapes, settlement dynamics, state structures, technological innovation, geography and power, and demography, ensuring that the limited essay offered here will benefit immensely from being considered in tandem with other *Cambridge Elements* in the Series.

References

Abbas, M. (2017). A survey of the military role of the Sherden warriors in the Egyptian army during the Ramesside period. *Égypte Nilotique et Méditerranéenne* **10**, 7–23.

Abell, N. (2014). Migration, mobility, and craftspeople in the Aegean Bronze Age: A case study from Ayia Irini on the island of Kea. *World Archaeology* **46** (**4**), 551–68.

Agouridis, C. (1997). Sea routes and navigation in the third millennium Aegean. *Oxford Journal of Archaeology* **16**, 1–24.

Agouridis, C. (1998). Οι μυλόλιθοι από το Πρωτοελλαδικό Φορτίο του Δοκού. *Enalia* **5**, 20–25.

Agouridis, C., & Michalis, M. (2021). The arduous voyage of underwater research during the recovery of the LBA shipwreck off Modi islet. In S. Demesticha & L. Blue, eds., *Under the Mediterranean I: Studies in Maritime Archaeology*. Leiden: Sidestone, pp. 23–42.

Aktypi, K. (2017). *The Mycenaean Cemetery of Agios Vasileios, Chalandritsa, in Achaea*. Oxford: Archaeopress.

Alberti, M. (2012). Aegean trade systems: Overview and observations on the Middle Bronze Age. In M. Alberti & S. Sabatini, eds., *Exchange Networks and Local Transformations: Interaction and Local Change in Europe and the Mediterranean from the Bronze Age to the Iron Age*. Oxford: Oxbow, pp. 22–43.

Alberti, M., Ascalone, E., & Peyronel, L., eds. (2006). *Weights in Context: Bronze Age Weighing Systems of Eastern Mediterranean*. Rome: Istituto Italiano di Numismatica.

Andreadaki-Vlazaki, M. (2015). Sacrifices in LM IIIB: Early Kydonian palatial centre. *Pasiphae* **9**, 27–42.

Angelopoulou, A. (2006). The lead seal and clay sealings. In L. Marangou, C. Renfrew, C. Doumas, & G. Gavalas, eds., *MAKRIANH AMOPΓOΥ – Makriani, Amorgos: An Early Bronze Age Fortified Settlement*. London: British School at Athens, pp. 219–22.

Archontidou-Argyri, A., & Kokkinoforou, M., eds. (2004). *Μύρινα της Πρώιμης Εποχής του Χαλκού*. Mytilene: Ministry of Culture.

Aruz, J. (2003). Art and interconnections in the third millennium B.C. In J. Aruz & R. Wallenfels, eds., *Art of the First Cities: The Third Millennium B.C. from the Mediterranean to the Indus*. New York: Metropolitan Museum of Art, pp. 239–50.

Aruz, J. (2008). *Marks of Distinction: Seals and Cultural Exchange between the Aegean and the Orient*. Mainz: Philipp von Zabern.

Barrett, C. (2009). The perceived value of Minoan and Minoanizing pottery in Egypt. *Journal of Mediterranean Archaeology* **22**(2), 211–34.

Bass, G. (1991). Evidence of trade from Bronze Age shipwrecks. In N. Gale, ed., *Bronze Age Trade in the Mediterranean*. Jonsered: P. Åströms Förlag, pp. 69–81.

Bass, G., & Hirschfeld, N. (2013). Return to Cape Gelidonya. *PASIPHAE: Rivista di Filologia e Antichità Egee* **7**, 99–104.

Bassiakos, Y., & Philaniotou, O. (2007). Early copper production on Kythnos: Archaeological evidence and analytical approaches to the reconstruction of the metallurgical process. In P. Day & R. Doonan, eds., *Metallurgy in the Early Bronze Age Aegean*. Oxford: Oxbow, pp. 19–56.

Becker, J., Jungfleisch, J., & von Rüden, C., eds. (2018). *Tracing Technoscapes: The Production of Bronze Age Wall Paintings of the Eastern Mediterranean*. Leiden: Sidestone Press.

Bekiaris, T., Chondrou, D., Ninou, I., & Valamoti, S.-M. (2020). Food-processing ground stone tools in the Greek Neolithic and Bronze Age: A synthesis of published data. *Journal of Greek Archaeology* **5**, 135–95.

Bell, C. (2006). *The Evolution of Long Distance Trading Relationships across the LBA/Iron Age Transition on the Northern Levantine Coast: Crisis, Continuity, and Change*. Oxford: Archaeopress.

Ben-Dor Evian, S., Yagel, O., Harlavan, Y., et al. (2021). Pharaoh's copper: The provenance of copper in bronze artifacts from post-imperial Egypt at the end of the second millennium BCE. *Journal of Archaeological Science: Reports* **38**, **103025**.

Ben-Shlomo, D., Nodarou, E., & Rutter, J. (2011). Transport stirrup jars from the southern Levant: New light on commodity exchange in the eastern Mediterranean. *American Journal of Archaeology* **115**, 329–53.

Bennett, J., & Halstead, P. (2014). O-no! Writing and righting redistribution. In D. Nakassis, J. Gulizio, & S. James, eds., *KE-RA-ME-JA: Studies Presented to Cynthia W. Shelmerdine*. Philadelphia: INSTAP, pp. 271–82.

Benzi, M. (2013). The southeast Aegean in the age of the Sea Peoples. In A. Killebrew & G. Lehmann, eds., *The Philistines and Other "Sea Peoples" in Text and Archaeology*. Atlanta: Society of Biblical Literature, pp. 509–42.

Berger, D., Soles, J., Giumlia-Mair, A., et al. (2019). Isotope systematics and chemical composition of tin ingots from Mochlos (Crete) and other Late Bronze Age sites in the Eastern Mediterranean sea: An ultimate key to tin provenance? *PLOS One* **14**(6), e0218326.

Betancourt, P., ed. (2006). *The Chrysokamino Metallurgy Workshop and Its Territory*. Princeton: American School of Classical Studies at Athens.

Bettelli, M. (2022). Specialization, exchanges, and socio-economic strategies of Italian Bronze Age Elites: The case of Aegean type pottery. In M. Frangipane, M. Poettinger, & B. Schefold, eds., *Ancient Economies in Comparative Perspective: Material Life, Institutions, and Economic Thought*. Cham: Springer, pp. 233–56.

Bevan, A. (2003). Reconstructing the role of Egyptian culture in the value regimes of the Bronze Age Aegean: Stone vessels and their social contexts. In R. Matthews & C. Roemer, eds., *Ancient Perspectives on Egypt*. London: Routledge, pp. 57–75.

Bevan, A. (2007). *Stone Vessels and Values in the Bronze Age Mediterranean*. Cambridge: Cambridge University Press.

Bevan, A., & Wilson, A. (2013). Models of settlement hierarchy based on partial evidence. *Journal of Archaeological Science* **40(5)**, 2415–27.

Bietak, M., Marinatos, N., & Palivou, C. (2007). *Taureador Scenes in Tell el-Dab'a (Avaris) and Knossos*. Vienna: Austrian Academy of Science.

Blackwell, N. (2014). Making the Lion Gate relief at Mycenae: Tool marks and foreign influence. *American Journal of Archaeology* **118(3)**, 451–88.

Blackwell, N. (2018). Contextualizing Mycenaean hoards: Metal control on the Greek mainland at the end of the Bronze Age. *American Journal of Archaeology* **122(4)**, 509–39.

Blake, E. (2014). *Social Networks and Regional Identity in Bronze Age Italy*. Cambridge: Cambridge University Press.

Bourdieu, P. (1990). *The Logic of Practice*, trans. R. Nice. Cambridge: Cambridge University Press.

Bowes, K. (2021). When Kuznets went to Rome: Roman economic well-being and the reframing of Roman history. *Capitalism: A Journal of History and Economics* **2(1)**, 7–40.

Braudel, F. (1972). *The Mediterranean and the Mediterranean World in the Age of Phillip II*, 2 vols., trans. S. Reynolds. London: Collins.

Broodbank, C. (1989). The longboat and society in the Cyclades and the Keros-Syros culture. *American Journal of Archaeology* **93(3)**, 319–37.

Broodbank, C. (2000). *An Island Archaeology of the Early Cyclades*. Cambridge: Cambridge University Press.

Broodbank, C. (2013). *The Making of the Middle Sea: A History of the Mediterranean from the Beginning to the Emergence of the Classical World*. London: Thames & Hudson.

Brughmans, T. (2013). Thinking through networks: A review of formal network methods in archaeology. *Journal of Archaeological Method and Theory* **20**, 623–62.

Buckley, S., Power, R., Andreadaki-Vlazaki, M., et al. (2021). Archaeometric evidence for the earliest exploitation of lignite from the Bronze Age eastern Mediterranean. *Nature: Scientific Reports* **11**, **24185**.

Burns, B. (2012). *Mycenaean Greece, Mediterranean Commerce, and the Formation of Identity.* Cambridge: Cambridge University Press.

Charalambous, A., & Webb, J. (2020). Metal procurement, artefact manufacture, and the use of imported tin bronze in Middle Bronze Age Cyprus. *Journal of Archaeological Science* **113**, **105047**.

Cherry, J. (2009). Sorting out Crete's prepalatial off-island interactions. In W. Parkinson & M. Galaty, eds., *Archaic State Interaction: The Eastern Mediterranean in the Bronze Age.* Santa Fe: Institute for Advanced Research Press, pp. 107–40.

Chliaoutakis, A., & Chalkiadakis, G. (2020). An agent-based model for simulating inter-settlement trade in past societies. *Journal of Artificial and Social Simulation* **23(3)**, 10.

Choleva, M. (2020). Travelling with the potter's wheel in the Early Bronze Age Aegean. *Annual of the British School at Athens* **115**, 59–104.

Cline, E. (1995). Egyptian and Near Eastern imports at Late Bronze Age Mycenae. In W. Vivian Davies & L. Schofield, eds., *Egypt, the Aegean, and the Levant: Interconnections in the Second Millennium BC.* London: British Museum Press, pp. 91–115.

Cline, E. (1998). Rich beyond the dreams of Avaris: Tell el-Dab'a and the Aegean world: A guide for the perplexed. *Annual of the British School at Athens* **93**, 199–219.

Cline, E., & Stannish, S. (2011). Sailing the great green sea? Amenhotep III's Aegean list from Kom el-Hetan, once more. *Journal of Ancient Egyptian Interconnections* **3(2)**, 6–16.

Colburn, C. (2008). Exotica and the Early Minoan elite: Eastern imports in prepalatial Crete. *American Journal of Archaeology* **112(2)**, 203–24.

Coldstream, J. N., & Catling, H. W., eds. (1996). *Knossos North Cemetery: Early Greek Tombs*, 2 vols. London: British School at Athens.

Cole, S. (2022). The Aegean and Egypt during the Fifteenth (Hyksos) Dynasty (1650–1550 BC) and beyond. In G. Miniaci & P. Lacovara, eds., *The Treasure of the Egyptian Queen Ahhotep.* London: Golden House, pp. 237–59.

Cucchi, T. (2008). Uluburun shipwreck stowaway house mouse: Molar shape analysis and indirect clues about the vessel's last journey. *Journal of Archaeological Science* **35**, 2953–59.

Cutler, J. (2019). Arachne's web: Women, weaving, and networks of knowledge in the Bronze Age Southern Aegean. *Annual of the British School at Athens* **114**, 79–92.

Cveček, S. (2020). Throwing their weights around? Anthropological perspectives on commodity and gift exchange at the dawn of the Early Bronze Age in western Anatolia. *Ägypten und Levante* **30**, 283–300.

D'Agata, A.-L., Girella, L., Papadopoulou, E., & Aquini, D., eds. (2022). *One State Many Worlds: Crete in the Late Minoan II–IIIA2 Early Period*. Rome: Quasar.

Dabney, M. (1996). Jewellery and seals. In J. Shaw & M. Shaw, eds., *Kommos I: The Kommos Region and Houses of the Minoan Town: Part 2: The Minoan Hilltop and Hillside Houses*. Princeton: American School of Classical Studies at Athens, pp. 263–69.

Davis, J., & Gorogianni, E. (2008). Potsherds from the edge: The construction of identities and the limits of Minoanized areas of the Aegean. In N. Brodie, J. Doole, G. Gavalas, & C. Renfrew, eds., *Horizon: A Colloquium on the Prehistory of the Cyclades*. Cambridge: McDonald Institute for Archaeological Research, pp. 339–48.

Dawson, H., & Nikolakopoulou, I. (2020). East meets west: Aegean identities and interactions in the Late Bronze Age Mediterranean. In D. Warburton, ed., *Political and Economic Interaction on the Edge of Early Empires*. Berlin: Exzellenzcluster 264 Topoi, pp. 155–92.

Day, P., Doumas, C., Erkanal, H., et al. (2009). New light on the "Kastri Group": A petrographic and chemical investigation of ceramics from Liman Tepe and Bekle Tepe. *Arkeometri Sonuçlari Toplantisi* **24**, 335–46.

Day, P., Hein, A., Kardamaki, E., et al. (2020). Maritime commodity trade from the Near East to the Mycenaean heartland: Canaanite jars in Final Palatial Tiryns. *Jahrbuch des Deutschen Archäologischen Instituts* **135**, 1–99.

Day, P., Quinn, P., Rutter, J., & Kilikoglou, V. (2011). A world of goods: Transport stirrup jars and commodity exchange at the Late Bronze Age harbour of Kommos, Crete. *Hesperia* **80**(4), 511–58.

Day, P., & Wilson, D. (2016). Dawn of the amphora: The emergence of maritime transport jars in the Early Bronze Age Aegean. In S. Demesticha & A. B. Knapp, eds., *Maritime Transport Containers in the Bronze–Iron Age Aegean and Eastern Mediterranean*. Uppsala: P. Åströms Förlag, pp. 17–37.

Dercksen, J. (2001). When we met in Hattuša: Trade according to the Old Assyrian Texts from Alishar and Boğazköy. In H. van Soldt, ed., *Veenhof Anniversary Volume: Studies Presented to Klaas R. Veenhof on the Occasion of his Sixty-Fifth Birthday*. Leiden: Nederlands Instituut voor het Nabije Oosten, pp. 39–66.

Dickinson, O. (2014). The Aegean. In C. Renfrew & P. Bahn, eds., *The Cambridge World Prehistory 3: Western and Central Asia*. Cambridge: Cambridge University Press, pp. 1860–84.

Dimopoulou, N. (1997). Workshops and craftsmen in the harbour town of Knossos at Poros-Katsambas. In R. Laffineur & P. Betancourt, eds., *TEXNH: Craftsmen, Craftswomen, and Craftsmanship in the Aegean Bronze Age*. Austin: University of Texas Press, pp. 433–38.

Donnelly, C. (2022). Cypro-Minoan abroad, Cypriots abroad? In G. Bourogiannis, ed., *Beyond Cyprus: Investigating Cypriot Connectivity in the Mediterranean from the Late Bronze Age to the End of the Classical Period*. Athens: National and Kapodistrian University of Athens, pp. 195–206.

Driessen, J. (2019). The Santorini eruption: An archaeological investigation of its distal impacts on Minoan Crete. *Quaternary International* **499**, 195–204.

Driessen, J., & Macdonald, C. (1997). *The Troubled Island: Minoan Crete before and after the Santorini Eruption*. Liège: University of Liège.

Eshel, T., Gilboa, A., Tirosh, O., Erel, Y., & Yahalom-Mack, N. (2023). The earliest silver currency hoards in the southern Levant: Metal trade in the transition from the Middle to the Late Bronze Age. *Journal of Archaeological Science* **149**, **105705**.

Evans, J., & Renfrew, C. (1968). *Excavations at Saliagos near Antiparos*. London: British School at Athens.

Fappas, I. (2012). Precious gifts and the circulation of oils in the ancient eastern Mediterranean. *Talanta* **44**, 157–82.

Foster, B. (2016). *The Age of Agade: Inventing Empire in Ancient Mesopotamia*. London: Routledge.

Frangipane, M. (2018). From a subsistence economy to the production of wealth in ancient formative societies: A political economy perspective. *Economia Politica* **35**(3), 677–89.

Galaty, M. (2018). Mycenaean glocalism: Greek political economies and international trade. In K. Kristiansen, T. Lindkvist, & J. Myrdal, eds., *Trade and Civilization: Economic Networks and Cultural Ties from Prehistory to the Early Modern Era*. Cambridge: Cambridge University Press, pp. 143–71.

Galaty, M., Nakassis, D., & Parkinson, W. A., eds. (2011). Redistribution in Aegean palatial societies. *American Journal of Archaeology* **115**(2), 175–244.

Gale, N. (2011). Copper oxhide ingots and lead isotope provenancing. In P. Betancourt & S. Ferrence, eds., *Metallurgy: Understanding How, Learning Why*. Philadelphia: INSTAP, pp. 213–30.

Gale, N., & Stos-Gale, Z. (1981). Cycladic lead and silver metallurgy. *Annual of the British School at Athens* **76**, 169–224.

Gale, N., & Stos-Gale, Z. (2008). Changing patterns in prehistoric Cycladic metallurgy. In N. Brodie, J. Doole, G. Gavalas, & C. Renfrew, eds., *Horizon: A Colloquium on the Prehistory of the Cyclades*. Cambridge: McDonald Institute for Archaeological Research, pp. 387–408.

Gauß, W., Klebinder-Gauss, G., Kiriatzi, E., Pentedeka, A., & Georgakopoulou, M. (2015). Aegina: An important center of production of cooking pottery from the prehistoric to the historic era. In M. Spataro & A. Villing, eds., *Ceramics, Cuisine, and Culture: The Archaeological and Science of Kitchen Pottery in the Ancient Mediterranean World*. Oxford: Oxbow, pp. 65–74.

Georgakopoulou, M. (2007). The metallurgical remains. In C. Renfrew, C. Doumas, L. Marangou, & G. Gavalas, eds., *Keros, Dhaskalio Kavos: The Investigations of 1987–1988*. Cambridge: McDonald Institute for Archaeological Research, pp. 380–401.

Georgakopoulou, M. (2016). Mobility and Early Bronze Age southern Aegean metal production. In E. Kiriatzi & C. Knappett, eds., *Human Mobility and Technology Transfer in the Prehistoric Mediterranean*. Cambridge: Cambridge University Press, pp. 46–67.

Georgiadis, M. (2003). *The South-Eastern Aegean in the Mycenaean Period: Islands, Landscape, Death, and Ancestors*. Oxford: Archaeopress.

Gestoso-Singer, G. (2015). Small ingots and scrap metal in the eastern Mediterranean during the Late Bronze Age. In J. Mynářová, P. Onderaka, & P. Pavúk, eds., *There and Back Again: The Crossroads II*. Prague: Charles University, pp. 85–127.

Giannopoulos, T. (2008). *Die Letzte Elite der Mykenischen Welt: Achaia im Mykenischen Zeit und das Phänomen der Kriegerbestattungen im 12.-11. Jahrhundert v. Chr.* Bonn: Habelt.

Girella, L. (2005). Ialysos: Foreign relations in the Late Bronze Age, a funerary perspective. In R. Laffineur & E. Greco, eds., *Emporia: Aegeans in the Central and Eastern Mediterranean*. Liège: University of Liège, pp. 129–39.

Glanville, S. (1931). Records of a royal dockyard at the time of Thutmose III: Papyrus British Museum 10056. *Zeitschrift für Ägyptische Sprache und Altertumskunde* **66**, 105–21.

Gorogianni, E., Cutler, J., & Fitzimons, R. (2015). Something old, something new: Non-local brides as catalysts for cultural exchange at Ayia Irini, Kea? In N. Stampolidis, Ç. Maner, & K. Kopanias, eds., *Nostoi: Indigenous Culture, Migration, and Integration in the Aegean Islands and Western Anatolia during the Late Bronze Age and Early Iron Age*. Istanbul: Koç University Press, pp. 889–922.

Gorogianni, E., Pavúk, P., & Girella, L., eds. (2016). *Beyond Thalassocracies: Understanding Processes of Minoanisation and Mycenaeanisation in the Aegean.* Oxford: Oxbow.

Graziadio, G. (1998). Trade circuits and trade-routes in the Shaft Grave period. *Studi Micenei ed Egeo-Anatolici* **40(1)**, 29–76.

Greif, A. (2006). *Institutions and the Path to the Modern Economy: Lessons from Medieval Trade.* Cambridge: Cambridge University Press.

Guichard, M. (2005). *La vaiselle de luxe de rois Mari: matériaux pour le dictionnaire de Babylonien de Paris.* Paris: Editions Recherche sur les Civilisations.

Gundacker, R. (2017). Papyrus British Museum 10056: Ergebnisse einer Neukollationierung und Anmerkungen zur inhaltlichen Auswertung im Rahmen der militärischen Ausbildung Amenophis' II. *Ägypten und Levant* **27**, 281–334.

Hadjianastasiou, O. (1998). Notes from Kythnos. In L. Mendoni & A. Mazarakis-Ainian, eds., *Kea-Kythnos: History and Archaeology.* Paris: de Boccard, pp. 259–73.

Hadjidaki-Marder, E. (2021). *The Minoan Shipwreck at Pseira, Crete.* Philadelphia: INSTAP.

Hallager, B. (2017). The LM IIIB settlements at Khania, West Crete. In C. Langohr, ed., *How Long is a Century? Late Minoan IIIB Pottery: Relative Chronology and Regional Differences.* Louvain: University of Louvain, pp. 37–52.

Hallager, E., & Hallager, B., eds. (2000). *The Greek Swedish Excavations at the Agia Aikaterini Square, Kastelli, Khania 1970–1987*, vol. 2. Stockholm: P. Åström.

Hallager, E., & Hallager, B., eds. (2003). *The Greek-Swedish Excavations at the Agia Aikaterini Square, Kastelli, Khania, 1970–1987 and 2001*, vol. 3. Stockholm: P. Åström.

Halstead, P. (1981). From determinism to uncertainty: Social storage and the rise of the Minoan palace. In A. Sheridan & G. Bailey, eds., *Economic Archaeology.* Oxford: Archaeopress, pp. 187–213.

Hartenberger, B., & Runnels, C. (2001). The organization of flaked stone production at Bronze Age Lerna. *Hesperia* **70**, 255–83.

Haskell, H., Jones, R., Day, P., & Killen, J. (2011). *Transport Stirrup Jars of the Bronze Age Aegean and East Mediterranean.* Philadelphia: INSTAP.

Helzer, M. (1989). Sinaranu, Son of Siginu, and the trade relations between Ugarit and Crete. *Minos* **24**, 7–28.

Hirschfeld, N. 2000. Marked Late Bronze Age Pottery from the Kingdom of Ugarit. In M. Yon, V. Karageorghis, & N. Hirschfeld, eds., *Céramiques*

Mycéniennes (Ras Shamra Ougarit 13). Nicosia: The A. G. Leventis Foundation, pp. 163–200.

Hirschfeld, N. (2004). Eastwards via Cyprus? The marked Mycenaean pottery of Enkomi, Ugarit, and Tell Abu Hawam. In J. Balensi, J.-Y. Monchambert, & S. Müller Celka, eds., *La Céramique mycénienne de l'Égée au Levant.* Lyon: de Boccard, pp. 97–103.

Horden, P., & Purcell, N. (2000). *The Corrupting Sea: A Study of Mediterranean History.* Oxford: Blackwell.

Ialongo, N. (2022). Weight-based trade and the formation of a global network: Material correlates of market exchange in pre-literate Bronze Age Europe (c. 2300–800 BC). In M. Frangipane, M. Poettinger, & B. Schefold, eds., *Ancient Economies in Comparative Perspective: Material Life, Institutions, Economic Thought.* Cham: Springer, pp. 207–32.

Ialongo, N., & Rahmstorf, L. (2019). The identification of balance-weights in pre-literate Bronze Age Europe: Typology, chronology, distribution, and metrology. In L. Rahmstorf & E. Stratford, eds., *Weights and Marketplaces.* Kiel: Wachholtz Murmann, pp. 105–26.

Jarriel, K. (2021). Climate disaster and the resilience of local maritime networks: Two examples from the Aegean Bronze Age. *Quaternary International* **597**, 118–30.

Jung, R. (2009). Pirates of the Aegean: Italy–the east Aegean–Cyprus at the end of the second millennium BC. In V. Karageorghis & O. Kouka, eds., *Cyprus and the East Aegean: Intercultural Contacts from 3000 to 500 BC.* Nicosia: The A.G. Leventis Foundation, pp. 72–93.

Jung, R. (2018). Warriors and weapons in the central and eastern Balkans. In S. Alexandrov, ed., *Gold and Bronze: Metals, Technologies, and Interregional Contacts in the Eastern Balkans during the Bronze Age.* Sofia: National Archaeological Institute and Museum, pp. 240–41.

Jung, R. (2021). Uneven and combined: Product exchange in the Mediterranean (3rd to 2nd millennium BCE). In S. Gimatzidis & R. Jung, eds., *The Critique of Archaeological Economy.* Cham: Springer, pp. 139–62.

Jung, R., & Mehofer, M. (2009). A sword of Naue II type from Ugarit and the historical significance of Italian-type weaponry in the eastern Mediterranean. *Aegean Archaeology* **8**, 111–35.

Jung, R., & Mehofer, M. (2013). Mycenaean Greece and Bronze Age Italy: Cooperation, trade, and war. *Archäologisches Korrespondenzblatt* **43(2)**, 175–93.

Jung, R., Moschos, I., & Mehofer, M. (2008). Φονεύοντας με τον Ίδιο Τρόπο: Οι Ειρηνικές Επαφές για τον Πόλεμο μεταξύ Δυτικής Ελλάδας και Ιταλίας κατά τη διάρκεια των Όψιμων Μυκηναϊκών Χρόνων. In S. Paipetis &

C. Giannopoulou, eds., *Πρακτικά: Πολιτισμική Αλληλογονιμοποίηση Νοτίας Ιταλίας και Δυτικής Ελλάδας μέσα από την Ιστορία*. Athens: Region of Western Greece, pp. 85–107.

Kakavogianni, O., Douni, K., & Nezeri, F. (2008). Silver metallurgical finds dating from the end of the Final Neolithic period until the Middle Bronze Age in the area of Mesogeia. In I. Tzachili, ed., *Aegean Metallurgy in the Bronze Age*. Athens: Ta Pragmata, pp. 45–57.

Kalogeropoulos, K. (2005). Decorative schemes as an indication of artistic relations between Early Mycenaean Greece and the eastern Mediterranean. In R. Laffineur & E. Greco, eds., *EMPORIA: Aegeans in the Central and Eastern Mediterranean*. Liège: University of Liège, pp. 393–403.

Karabatsoli, A. (2011). The chipped stone industry. In D. Pullen, ed., *Nemea Valley Archaeological Project 1: The Early Bronze Age Village on Tsoungiza Hill*. Princeton: American School of Classical Studies at Athens, pp. 661–726.

Karageorghis, V., Kanta, A., Stampolidis, N. C., & Sakellarakis, Y., eds. (2014). *Kypriaka in Crete: From the Bronze Age to the End of the Archaic Period*. Nicosia: The A.G. Leventis Foundation.

Karageorghis, V., & Marketou, T. (2006). Late Bronze Age IA/IB Rhodian imitations of Cypriote ceramics: The evidence from Trianda (Ialysos). In E. Czerny, I. Hein, H. Hunger, D. Melman, & A. Schwab, eds., *Timelines: Studies in Honor of Manfred Bietak*. Leuven: Peeters, pp. 455–69.

Kardulias, P. N. (1999). Multiple levels in the Aegean Bronze Age world-system. In P. Kardulias, ed., *World Systems Theory in Practice: Leadership, Production, and Exchange*. Oxford: Rowman & Littlefield, pp. 179–201.

Kardulias, P. N., & Runnels, C. (1995). The lithic artifacts: Flaked stone and other nonflaked lithics. In C. Runnels, D. Pullen, & S. Langdon, eds., *Artifact and Assemblage: The Finds from a Regional Survey of the Southern Argolid, Greece: Vol. 1: The Prehistoric and Early Iron Age Pottery and the Lithic Artifacts*. Stanford: Stanford University Press, pp. 74–139.

Kassianidou, V. (2014). Appendix II: Oxhide ingots made of Cypriot copper found in Crete. In V. Karageorghis, A. Kanta, N. Stampolidis, & Y. Sakellarakis, eds., *Kypriaka in Crete from the Bronze Age to the End of the Archaic Period*. Nicosia: The A.G. Leventis Foundation, pp. 307–11.

Kayafa, M. (1999). *Bronze Age Metallurgy in the Peloponnese, Greece*. Ph.D. dissertation. Birmingham: University of Birmingham.

Kelder, J. (2022). From Thutmose III to Homer to Blackadder: Egypt, the Aegean, and the "barbarian periphery" of the Late Bronze Age world system. In J. Spier & S. Cole, eds., *Egypt and the Classical World: Cross-Cultural Encounters in Antiquity*. Los Angeles: J. Paul Getty Museum, pp. 4–14.

Kiderlen, M., Bode, M., Hauptmann, A., & Bassiakos, Y. (2016). Tripod cauldrons produced at Olympia give evidence for trade with copper from Faynan (Jordan) to south west Greece, c. 950–750 BCE. *Journal of Archaeological Science: Reports* **8**, 303–13.

Kilian-Dirlmeier, I. (1997). *Das Middelbronzezeitliche Schachtgrab von Ägina*. Mainz: Philipp von Zabern.

Kislev, M., Artzy, M., & Marcus, E. (1993). Import of an Aegean food plant to a Middle Bronze IIA coastal site in Israel. *Levant* **25(1)**, 145–54.

Knapp, A. (2011). Cyprus, copper, and Alashiya. In P. Betancourt & S. Ferrence, eds., *Metallurgy: Understanding How, Learning Why*. Philadelphia: INSTAP, pp. 249–54.

Knapp, A. B. (2018). *Seafaring and Seafarers in the Bronze Age Eastern Mediterranean*. Brill: Leiden.

Knapp, A. (2022). Bronze Age Cyprus and the Aegean: "Exotic currency" and objects of connectivity. *Journal of Greek Archaeology* **7**, 67–93.

Knapp, A., & Manning, S. (2016). Crisis in context: The end of the Late Bronze Age in the eastern Mediterranean. *American Journal of Archaeology* **120(1)**, 99–149.

Knapp, A., & Meyer, N. (2023). Merchants and mercantile society on Late Bronze Age Cyprus. *American Journal of Archaeology* **127(3)**, 309–38.

Knappett, C. (2016). Networks in archaeology: Between scientific method and humanistic metaphor. In T. Brughmans, A. Collar, & F. Coward, eds., *The Connected Past: Challenges to Network Studies in Archaeology and History*. Oxford: Oxford University Press, pp. 21–34.

Knappett, C., Evans, T., & Rivers, R. (2008). Modelling maritime interaction in the Aegean Bronze Age. *Antiquity* **82**, 1009–24.

Knappett, C., & Nikolakopoulou, I. (2008). Colonialism without colonies? A Bronze Age case study from Akrotiri, Thera. *Hesperia* **77(1)**, 1–42.

Knappett, C., Rivers, R., & Evans, T. (2011). The Theran eruption and Minoan palatial collapse: New interpretations gained from modelling the maritime network. *Antiquity* **85**, 1008–23.

Knodell, A. (2021). *Societies in Transition in Early Greece: An Archaeological History*. Oakland: University of California Press.

Koehl, R. (2005). Preliminary observations on the unpublished Mycenaean pottery from Woolley's dig-hosue at Tell Atchana. In R. Laffineur & E. Greco, eds., *Emporia: Aegeans in the Central and Eastern Mediterranean*. Belgium: Kliemo, pp. 415–22.

Konsolaki-Yannopoulou, E. (2019). Ναυτικό εμπόριο στο πέτρινο Λιοντάρι του Πόρου. Ο Υστερομυκηναϊκός οικισμός στη βραχονησίδα Μόδι. *ΑΡΧΑΙΟΛΟΓΙΑ ΚΑΙ ΤΕΧΝΕΣ* **131**, 56–67.

Kostoula, M. (2000). Die frühhelladischen Tonplomben mit Siegelabdrücken aus Petri bei Nemea. In I. Pini, ed., *Minoisch-mykenische Glyptik. Stil, Ikonographie, Funktion*. Berlin: Gebr. Mann Verlag, pp. 135–48.

Kostoula, M., & Maran, J. (2012). A group of animal-headed faience vessels from Tiryns. In M. Gruber, S. Ahituv, G. Lehmann, & Z. Talshir, eds., *All the Wisdom of the East: Studies in Near Eastern Archaeology and History in Honor of Eliezer D. Oren*. Fribourg and Göttingen: Academic Press and Vandenhoeck & Ruprecht, pp. 193–234.

Kotsonas, A., ed. (2014). *Understanding Standardization and Variation in Mediterranean Ceramics: Mid 2nd to Late 1st Millennium BC*. Leuven: Peeters.

Laffineur, R. (1998). From west to east: The Aegean and Egypt in the early Late Bronze Age. In E. Cline & D. Harris-Cline, eds., *The Aegean and the Orient in the Second Millennium*. Liège: University of Liège, pp. 53–67.

Lankton, J., Pulak, C., & Gratuze, B. (2022). Glass ingots from the Uluburun shipwreck: Glass by the batch in the Late Bronze age. *Journal of Archaeological Science: Reports* **42, 103354**.

Legarra Herrero, B. (2011). New kid on the block: The nature of the first systemic contacts between Crete and the eastern Mediterranean around 2000 BC. In T. Wilkinson, S. Sherratt, & J. Bennet, eds., *Interweaving Worlds: Systemic Interactions in Eurasia, 7th to 1st Millennia BC*. Oxford: Oxbow, pp. 266–81.

Legarra Herrero, B. (2014). The role of gold in south Aegean exchange networks (3100–1800). In H. Meller, R. Risch, & E. Pernicka, eds., *Metalle der Macht: Frühes Gold und Silber*. Halle: Landesmuseum für Vorgeschichte, pp. 467–82.

Lehner, J., Kuruçaıyırlı, E., & Hirschfeld, N. (2020). Oxhides, buns, bits, and pieces: Analyzing the ingot cargo of the Cape Gelidonya shipwreck. In A. Gilboa & A. Yasur-Landau, eds., *Nomads of the Mediterranean*. Leiden: Brill, pp. 161–76.

Leurquin, K. (1986). Chipped stone analysis 1975–1982. In M. Joukowsky, ed., *Prehistoric Aphrodisias: An Account of the Excavations and Artifact Studies*. Providence: Brown University, pp. 240–85.

Lilyquist, C. (1996). Stone vessels at Kamid el-Loz, Lebanon: Egyptian, Egyptianizing, or Non-Egyptian? A question at sites from the Sudan to Iraq to the Greek mainland. In R. Hachmann, ed., *Kamid el-Loz 16: Schatzhaus: Studien*. Bonn: Habelt, pp. 133–73.

Lis, B. (2018). Potters in captivity? An alternative explanation for the Italo-Mycenaean pottery of the 13th century BC. In J. Driessen, ed., *An Archaeology of Forced Migration: Crisis-Induced Mobility and the*

Collapse of the 13th c. BC Eastern Mediterranean. Louvain: University of Louvain, pp. 261–72.

Lis, B., Mommsen, H., Maran, J., & Prillwitz, S. (2020). Investigating pottery production and consumption patterns at the Late Mycenaean cemetery of Perati. *Journal of Archaeological Sciences: Reports* **32**, 102453.

Lis, B., Mommsen, H., & Sterba, J. (2023). Production and distribution of White Ware towards the end of Late Bronze Age in Greece. *Journal of Archaeological Science: Reports* **47**, 103812.

Lloyd, S., & Mellaart, J. (1962). *Beycesultan I: The Chalcolithic and Early Bronze Age Layers*. Ankara: British Institute of Archaeology at Ankara.

Ludvik, G., Kenoyer, J., Pieniążek, M., & Aylward, W. (2015). New perspectives on stone bead technology at Bronze Age Troy. *Anatolian Studies* **65**, 1–18.

Mackenzie, D. (1904). The successive settlements at Phylakopi in their Aegeo-Cretan relations. In T. Atkinson, ed., *Excavations at Phylakopi in Melos*. London: MacMillan, pp. 238–72.

Mahler-Slasky, Y., & Kislev, M. (2010). Lathyrus consumption in Late Bronze and Iron Age sites in Israel: An Aegean affinity. *Journal of Archaeological Science* **37(10)**, 2477–85.

Malamat, A. (1998). *Mari and the Bible*. Leiden: Brill.

Maran, J. (1998). *Kulturwandel auf dem griechischen Festland und den Kykladen im späten 3. Jahrtausend v. Chr.* Bonn: Habelt.

Maran, J. (2004). The spreading of objects and ideas in the Late Bronze Age eastern Mediterranean: Two case examples from the Argolid of the 13th and 12th centuries B.C. *Bulletin of the American Society for Oriental Research* **336**, 11–30.

Maran, J. (2007). Sea-borne contacts between the Aegean, the Balkans, and the Central Mediterranean in the 3rd Millennium BC: The unfolding of the Mediterranean world. In I. Galanaki, H. Tomas, Y. Galanakis, & R. Laffineur, eds., *Between the Aegean and Baltic Seas: Prehistory across Borders*. Liège: University of Liège, pp. 3–21.

Maran, J. (2011). Evidence for Levantine religious practice in the Late Bronze Age Sanctuary of Phylakopi on Melos? *Eretz Israel* **30**, 65–73.

Maran, J., & Kostoula, M. (2014). The spider's web: Innovation and society in the Early Helladic period of the corridor houses. In Y. Galanakis, T. Wilkinson, & J. Bennet, eds., *ΑΘΥΡΜΑΤΑ: Critical Essays on the Archaeology of the Eastern Mediterranean in Honour of E. Susan Sherratt*. Oxford: Archaeopress, pp. 141–58.

Maran, J., & Papadimitriou, A. (2021). Der lange Schatten der Palastzeit: Die nördliche Unterstadt von Tiryns: ein Großbauprojekt palast-und nachpalast-zeitlicher Entscheidungsträger. *Archäologischer Anzeiger* **2021**, 1–141.

Marketou, T. (2014). Time and space in the Middle Bronze Age Aegean world: Ialysos (Rhodes), a gateway to the eastern Mediterranean. In S. Souvatzi, & A. Hadji, eds., *Space and Time in Mediterranean Prehistory*. London: Routledge, pp. 176–95.

Markowitz, Y., & Lacovara, P. (2009). Egypt and the Aigina treasure. In J. Lesley Fitton, ed., *The Aigina Treasure: Aegean Bronze Age Jewellery and a Mystery Revisited*. London: British Museum Press, pp. 59–60.

Matricardi, E., Jung, R., Mommsen, H., Pacciarelli, M., & Sterba, J. (2021). Aegean-type and Aegeanizing pottery from Ionian Apulia: New studies and provenance analyses. *Origini* **44**, 111–48.

Maxwell-Hyslop, K. (1971). *Western Asiatic Jewellery c. 3000–612 B.C.* London: Methuen.

Menelaou, S. (2020). Beyond networks and macro-scale analysis: Unravelling micro-histories of pottery at Early Bronze Age Samos, Greece through an integrated methodology. *Proceedings of the International Scientific Conference, Methodology and Archaeometry* **6**, 57–74.

Menelaou, S. (2021). Insular, marginal, or multiconnected? Maritime interaction and connectivity in the East Aegean islands during the Early Bronze Age through ceramic evidence. In L. Dierksmeier, F. Schön, A. Kouremenos, A. Condit, & V. Palmowski, eds., *European Islands between Isolated and Interconnected Life Worlds: Interdisciplinary Long-Term Perspectives*. Tübingen: Tübingen University Press, pp. 131–63.

Merrillees, R. (2003). The first appearances of Kamares Ware in the Levant. *Ägypten und Levante* **13**, 127–42.

Michailidou, A. (1990). The lead weights from Akrotiri: The archaeological record. In D. Hardy, C. Doumas, J. Sakellarakis, & P. Warren, eds., *Thera and the Aegean World III*. London: The Thera Foundation, pp. 407–19.

Michailidou, A., & Voutsa, K. (2005). Humans as a commodity in Aegean and Oriental societies. In R. Laffineur & E. Greco, eds., *EMPORIA: Aegeans in the Central and Eastern Mediterranean*. Liège: University of Liège, pp. 17–28.

Mommsen, H., Beier, T., Diehl, U., & Podzuweit, C. (1992). Provenance determination of Mycenaean sherds found in Tell el Amarna by neutron activation analysis. *Journal of Archaeological Science* **19**(3), 295–302.

Monroe, C. (2009). *Scales of Fate: Trade, Tradition, and Transformation in the Eastern Mediterranean ca. 1350–1175 BCE*. Münster: Ugarit Verlag.

Monroe, C. (2020). Sunk costs at Late Bronze Age Uluburun. *Bulletin of the American Schools of Oriental Research* **357**, 19–33.

Moran, W. (2002). *The Amarna Letters*. Baltimore: Johns Hopkins University Press.

Morero, E., & Prévalet, R. (2015). Technological transfer of luxury craftsmanship between Crete and the Orient during the Bronze Age. In J. Mynářova, P. Onderka, & P. Pavúk, eds., *There and Back Again: The Crossroads II.* Prague: Charles University, pp. 59–83.

Morgan, L. (2010). An Aegean Griffin in Egypt: The Hunt Frieze at Tell el Dabᶜa. *Ägypten und Levante* **20**, 303–23.

Morrison, J., Nodarou, E., & Cutler, J. (2022). Vessels and loom weights: Tracing southeast Aegean connections at Neopalatial Mochlos. In J. Murphy & J. Morrison, eds., *Kleronomia: Legacy and Inheritance: Studies on the Aegean Bronze age in Honor of Jeffrey S. Soles.* Philadelphia: INSTAP, pp. 155–71.

Mountjoy, P. (2018). *Decorated Pottery in Cyprus and Philistia in the 12th Century BC: Cypriot IIIC and Philistine IIIC*, 2 vols. Vienna: Austrian Academy of Sciences Press.

Mountjoy, P., & Mommsen, H. (2001). Mycenaean pottery from Qantir-Piramesse, Egypt. *Annual of the British School at Athens* **96**, 123–55.

Mountjoy, P., & Mommsen, H. (2015). Neutron activation analysis of Aegean-Style IIIC pottery from 11 Cypriot and various Near Eastern Sites. *Ägypten und Levante* **25**, 421–508.

Muhs, B. (2016). *The Ancient Egyptian Economy: 3000–30 BCE.* Cambridge: Cambridge University Press.

Murray, S. (2017). *The Collapse of the Mycenaean Economy: Imports, Trade, and Institutions 1300–700 BC.* Cambridge: Cambridge University Press.

Murray, S. (2020). Merchants, cultural boundaries, and orderly interaction in the Late Bronze and Early Iron Age Mediterranean. In J. Driessen & A. Vanzetti, eds., *Communication Uneven: Acceptance of and Resistance to Foreign Influence in the Connected Ancient Mediterranean.* Louvain: University of Louvain, pp. 203–12.

Murray, S. (2022). Aegean consumption of Egyptian material culture in the sixteenth century BC: Objects, iconography, and interpretation. In G. Miniaci & P. Lacovara, eds., *The Treasure of the Egyptian Queen Ahhotep.* London: Golden House Press, pp. 261–70.

Murray, S., Godsey, M., Frankl, J., et al. (2022). The Bays of East Attica Regional Survey 2020–2021: New evidence for settlement, production, and exchange in Porto Rafti, Greece, from prehistory to Late Antiquity. *Mouseion* **19**, 112–74.

Nafplioti, A. (2009). Mycenae revisited part 2: Exploring the local versus non-local geographical origin of the individuals from Grave Circle A: Evidence from strontium isotope ratio (87Sr/86 Sr) analysis. *Annual of the British School at Athens* **104**, 279–91.

Nakassis, D., Galaty, M., & Parkinson, W., eds. (2016). Discussion and debate: Reciprocity in Aegean palatial societies: Gifts, debt, and the foundations of economic exchange. *Journal of Mediterranean Archaeology* **29** (**1**), 61–132.

Nerantzis, N., & Papadopoulos, S. (2013). Reassessment and new date on the diachronic relationship of Thassos island with its indigenous metal resources: A review. *Archaeological and Anthropological Sciences* **5**, 183–96.

Niemeier, B., & Niemeier, W.-D. (2000). Aegean frescoes in Syria-Palestine: Alalakh and Tel Kabri. In S. Sherratt, ed., *The Wall Paintings of Thera*. Athens: Thera Foundation, pp. 763–802.

Nikita, K., & Henderson, J. (2006). Glass analysis from Mycenaean Thebes and Elateia: Compositional evidence for a Mycenaean glass industry. *Journal of Glass Studies* **48**, 71–120.

Nikita, K., Henderson, J., & Nightingale, G. (2009). An archaeological and scientific study of Mycenaean glass from Elateia-Alonaki, Greece. In K. Janssens, P. Degryse, P. Cosyns, J. Caen, & L. Van't Dack, eds., *Annales du 17e Congrès de l'Association Interntionale pour l'Histoire du Verre*. Antwerp: University Press of Antwerp, pp. 39–46.

Nikolakopoulou, I. (2009). Beware Cretans bearing gifts: Tracing the origins of Minoan influence at Akrotiri, Thera. In C. Macdonald, E. Hallager, & W.-D. Niemeier, eds., *The Minoans in the Central, Eastern, and Northern Aegean: New Evidence*. Athens: Danish Institute at Athens, pp. 31–39.

Nikolakopoulou, I., & Knappett, C. (2016). Mobilities in the Neopalatial southern Aegean: The case of Minoanization. In E. Kiriatzi & C. Knappett, eds., *Human Mobility and Technological Transfer in the Prehistoric Mediterranean*. Cambridge: Cambridge University Press, pp. 102–15.

North, D. (2005). *Understanding the Process of Economic Change*. Princeton: Princeton University Press.

Nosch, M.-L. (2014). Mycenaean wool economies in the latter part of the second millennium BC Aegean. In C. Breniquet & C. Michel, eds., *Wool Economy in the Ancient Near East and the Aegean*. Oxford: Oxbow, pp. 371–400.

Numrich, M., Schwall, C., Lockhoff, N., et al. (2023). Portable laser ablation sheds light on Early Bronze Age gold treasures in the Old World: New insights from Troy, Poliochni, and related finds. *Journal of Archaeological Science* **149**, **105694**.

Olsen, B. (2014). *Women in Mycenaean Greece: The Linear B Tablets from Pylos and Knossos*. London: Routledge.

Öniz, H. (2019). A new Bronze Age shipwreck with ingots in the west of Antalya: Preliminary results. *Palestine Exploration Quarterly* **151**, 3–14.

Palaima, T. (2014). Pylos tablet Vn 130 and the Pylos perfume industry. In D. Nakassis, J. Gulizio, & S. James, eds., *KE-RA-ME-JA: Studies Presented to Cynthia Shelmerdine*. Philadelphia: INSTAP, pp. 83–90.

Palaiologou, H. (2013). Late Helladic IIIC cremation burials at Chania of Mycenae. In M. Lochner & F. Ruppenstein, eds., *Brandbesttatungen von der mittleren Donau bis zur Ägäis zwischen 1300 und 750 v. Chr.* Vienna: Austrian Academy of Sciences, pp. 249–80.

Panagiotopoulos, D. (2001). Keftiu in context: Theban tomb paintings as a historical source. *Oxford Journal of Archaeology* **20**, 263–83.

Pantazis, T., Karydas, A., Doumas, C., et al. (2003). X-Ray fluorescence analysis of a gold ibex and other artifacts from Akrotiri. In K. Foster & R. Laffineur, eds., *METRON: Measuring the Aegean Bronze Age*. Liège: University of Liège, pp. 155–65.

Papadimitriou, N. (2012). Regional or "international" networks? A comparative examination of Aegean and Cypriot imported pottery in the Eastern Mediterranean. In A. Papadopoulos, ed., *TALANTA: Proceedings of the Dutch Archaeological and Historical Society* **44**, 92–136.

Papadimitriou, N. (2020). Προϊστορική εγκατάσταση στον Θορικό Αττικής: η συμβολή των ανασκαφών του Βαλέριου Στάη (1888, 1890, 1893). *Archaeologike Ephemeris* **159**, 149–254.

Papadimitriou, N. (2022). Cyprus and the Aegean in the Late Bronze Age. In G. Bourogiannis, ed., *Beyond Cyprus: Investigating Cypriot Connectivity in the Mediterranean from the Late Bronze Age to the End of the Classical Period*. Athens: National and Kapodistrian University of Athens, pp. 179–94.

Papadopoulos, J. (2001). Magna Achaia: Akhaian Late Geometric and Archaic pottery in South Italy and Sicily. *Hesperia* **70**, 373–460.

Papadopoulou, Z. (2011). Akrotiraki and Skali: New evidence for EBA lead/silver and copper production from southern Siphnos. In P. Betancourt & S. Ferrence, eds., *Metallurgy: Understanding How, Learning Why*. Philadelphia: INSTAP, pp. 149–56.

Parkinson, W. (2010). Beyond the peer: Social interaction and political evolution in the Bronze Age Aegean. In D. Pullen, ed., *Political Economies of the Aegean Bronze Age*. Oxford: Oxbow, pp. 11–34.

Parkinson, W. A., & Galaty, M. (2007). Secondary states in perspective: An integrated approach to state formation in the prehistoric Aegean. *American Anthropologist* **109**(1), 113–29.

Parkinson, W. A., & Galaty, M., eds., (2009). *Archaic State Interaction: The Eastern Mediterranean in the Bronze Age*. Santa Fe: Institute for Advanced Research Press.

Parkinson, W. A., Nakassis, D., & Galaty, M., eds. (2013). Forum: Crafts, specialists, and markets in Mycenaean Greece. *American Journal of Archaeology* **117**(3), 453–59.

Parlama, K. (2007). Παλαμάρι Σκύρου. Παρατηρήσεις στην εξέλιξη του οικισμού κατά την 3 η π.Χ. χιλιετία και προβλήματα αστικοποίησης. In E. Simantoni-Bournia, A. Laimou, L. Mendoni, & N. Kourou, eds., *Αμύμονα Έργα*. Athens: University of Athens, pp. 25–48.

Phelps, W., Lolos, Y., & Vichos, Y. (1999). *The Point Iria Wreck: Interconnections in the Mediterranean ca. 1200 BC*. Athens: Hellenic Institute of Marine Archaeology.

Phillips, J. (2007). The Amenhotep III "Plaques" from Mycenae: Comparison, contrast, and a question of chronology. In M. Bietak & E. Czerny, eds., *The Synchronization of Civilisations in the Second Millennium BC*. Vienna: Austrian Academy of Sciences, pp. 479–93.

Phillips, J. (2008). *Aegyptiaca on the Island of Crete in their Chronological Context: A Critical Review*, vols. I–II. Vienna: Austrian Academy of Sciences.

Phillips, J., & E. Cline. (2005). Amenhotep III and Mycenae: New evidence. In A. Dakouri-Hild & S. Sherratt, eds., *Autochthon: Papers Presented to O.T.P.K Dickinson on the Occasion of His Retirement*. Oxford: Archaeopress, pp. 317–28.

Polikreti, K., Murphy, J., Kantarelou, V., & Karydas. A. (2011). XRF analysis of glass beads from the Mycenaean palace of Nestor at Pylos, Peloponnesus, Greece: New insight into the LBA glass trade. *Journal of Archaeological Science* **38**, 2889–96.

Powell, W., Frachetti, M., Pulak, C., et al. (2022). Tin from Uluburun Shipwreck shows small-scale commodity exchange fueled continental tin supply across Late Bronze Age Eurasia. *Science Advances* **8**, **eabq3766**.

Pulak, C. (2008). The Uluburun Shipwreck and Late Bronze Age trade. In J. Aruz, K. Benzel, & J. Evans, eds., *Beyond Babylon: Art, Trade, and Diplomacy in the Second Millennium B.C.* New York and New Haven: Metropolitan Museum of Art and Yale University Press, pp. 289–310.

Pullen, D., ed. (2010). *Political Economies of the Aegean Bronze Age*. Oxford: Oxbow.

Pullen, D. (2021). Merchants, ports, and market exchange: Strategies for coping in an interconnected Mycenaean World. In J. Driessen & A. Vanzetti, eds., *Communication Uneven: Acceptance of and Resistance to Foreign Influences in the Connected Ancient Mediterranean*. Louvain-la-Neuve: University of Louvain, pp. 189–202.

Pullen, D. (2023). Coastscapes, small worlds, and maritime interactions in the Final Neolithic and Early Bronze Age Aegean. In V. Şahoğlu, I. Tuğcu, O. Kouka, et al., eds. *Hayat: A Life Dedicated to Archaeology*. Ankara: University of Ankara, pp. 335–51.

Quack, J. F. (2022). Altägyptische Amulette und ihre Handhabung. In A. Berlejung, N. Heeßel, & J. Quack, eds., *Orientalische Religionen in der Antike 31*. Tübingen: Tübingen University Press.

Rahmstorf, L. (2003). The identification of Early Helladic weights and their wider implications. In S. Foster & R. Laffineur, eds., *Metron: Measuring the Aegean Bronze Age*. Liège: University of Liège, pp. 293–300.

Rahmstorf, L. (2010). The concept of weighing during the Bronze Age in the Aegean, the Near East, and Europe. In I. Morley & C. Renfrew, eds., *The Archaeology of Measurement: Comprehending Heaven, Earth, and Time in Ancient Societies*. Cambridge: Cambridge University Press, pp. 88–105.

Rahmstorf, L. (2011). Maß für Maß. Indikatoren für Kulturkontakte im 3. Jahrtausend. In C. Hattler, ed., *Kykladen. Lebenswelten einer frühgriechischen Kultur*. Karlsruhe, Darmstadt: Primus Verlag, pp. 144–53.

Rahmstorf, L. (2015). The Aegean before and after c. 2200 BC between Europe and Asia: Trade as a prime mover of cultural change. In H. Meller, H. Wolfgang Arz, R. Jung, & R. Risch, eds., *2200 BC: Ein Klimasturz als Ursache für den Zerfall der Alten Welt?* Halle: Landesmuseum für Vorgeschichte, pp. 149–80.

Rahmstorf, L. (2016). Emerging economic complexity in the Aegean and western Anatolia during earlier third millennium BC. In B. Molloy, ed., *Of Odysseys and Oddities: Scales and Modes of Interaction between Prehistoric Aegean Societies and their Neighbors*. Oxford: Oxbow, pp. 225–76.

Rambach, J. (2000). *Kykladen I-II, Die Frühe Bronzezeit, Beiträge zur ur- und frühgeschichtlichen Archäologie des Mittelmeer-Kulturraumes 33–34*. Bonn: Habelt.

Renfrew, C. (1972). *The Emergence of Civilisation: The Cyclades and the Aegean in the Third Millennium BC*. London: Methuen.

Renfrew, C., Cann, J., & Dixon, J. (1965). Obsidian in the Aegean. *Annual of the British School at Athens* **60**, 225–47.

Rheinholdt, C. (2008). *Der frühbronzezeitliche Schmuckhortfnd von Kap Kolonna: Ägina und die Ägäis im Goldzeitalter des 3. Jahrtausends v. Chr.* Vienna: Austrian Academy of Sciences.

Roux, V., & Courty, M. (1998). Identification of wheel-fashioning: Technological analysis of 4th–3rd millennium BC oriental ceramics. *Journal of Archaeological Science* **25**, 747–63.

Rutter, J. (2006). Ceramic imports of the Neopalatial and Late Bronze Age eras. In J. Shaw & M. Shaw, eds., *Kommos V: The Monumental Buildings at Kommos*. Princeton: American School of Classical Studies at Athens, pp. 646–88.

Rutter, J. (2012). Migrant drinking assemblages in Aegean Bronze Age settings. In J. Maran & P. Stockhammer, eds., *Materiality and Social Practice: Transformative Capacities of Intercultural Encounters*. Oxford: Oxbow, pp. 73–88.

Rutter, J. (2014). The Canaanite transport amphora within the Late Bronze Age Aegean: A 2013 perspective on a frequently changing picture. In D. Nakassis, J. Gulizio, & S. James, eds., *KE-RA-ME-JA: Studies Presented to Cynthia W. Shelmerdine*. Philadelphia: INSTAP, pp. 53–69.

Sampson, A. (1988). *Μάνικα ΙΙ: Ο πρωτοελλαδικός οικισμός και το νεκροταφείο*. Athens: Community of Chalkis Editions.

Sauvage, C. (2012). *Routes maritimes et systèmes d'échanges internationaux au Bronze récent en Méditerranée orientale*. Lyon: Jean Pouilloux.

Schofield, L., & Parkinson, R. (1994). Of helmets and heretics: A possible Egyptian representation of Mycenaean warriors on a papyrus from El-Amarna. *The Annual of the British School at Athens* **89**, 157–70.

Schon, R. (2015). Weight sets: Identification and analysis. *Cambridge Archaeological Journal* **25**, 477–94.

Serpetsidaki, I. (2012). Πρόσφατη ανασκαφική έρευνα στον Πόρο – Κατσαμπά Ηρακλείου. In E. Andrianakis, P. Barthatilou, & I. Tzachili, eds., *Αρχαιολογικό Έργο Κρήτης 2*. Rethymno: University of Crete, pp. 164–72.

Shaw, J., & Blackman, D. (2020). Storage shipsheds at Kommos: Reviewed. *International Journal of Nautical Archaeology* **49(2)**, 406–11.

Shelmerdine, C. (1995). Shining and fragrant cloth in Homeric epic. In J. Carter & S. Morris, eds., *The Ages of Homer: A Tribute to Emily Townsend Vermeule*. Austin: University of Texas Press, pp. 99–107.

Shelmerdine, C. (1998). Where do we go from here? And how can the Linear B tablets help us get there? In E. Cline & D. Harris-Cline, eds., *The Aegean and the Orient in the Second Millennium*. Liège: University of Liège, pp. 291–99.

Sherratt, A. (1993). Who are you calling peripheral? Dependence and independence in European prehistory. In C. Scarre & F. Healy, eds., *Trade and Exchange in Prehistoric Europe*. Oxford: Oxbow, pp. 245–55.

Sherratt, A., & Sherratt, S. (1991). From luxuries to commodities: The nature of Mediterranean Bronze Age trading systems. In N. Gale, ed., *Bronze Age Trade in the Mediterranean: Papers Presented at the Conference Held at the Rewley House, Oxford, in December 1989*. Jonsered: P. Åströms Verlag, pp. 351–86.

Sherratt, S. (1994). Comments on Ora Negbi, the "Libyan Landscape" from Thera: A review of Aegean enterprises overseas in the Late Minoan IA period. *Journal of Mediterranean Archaeology* **7(2)**, 237–40.

Sherratt, S. (1999). E pur si muove: Pots, Markets, and Values in the Second Millennium Mediterranean. In J. P. Crielaard, V. Stissi, & G. van Wijngaarden, eds., *The Complex Past of Pottery: Production, Circulation, and Consumption of Mycenaean and Greek Pottery.* Amsterdam: Geiben, pp. 163–211.

Sherratt, S. (2003). The Mediterranean economy: "Globalization" at the end of the second millennium BCE. In W. Dever, & S. Gitin, eds., *Symbiosis, Symbolism, and the Power of the Past: Canaan, Ancient Israel, and their Neighbors from the Late Bronze Age through Roman Palestina.* Winona Lake: Eisenbrauns, pp. 37–62.

Sienkiewicz, J. (2022). Social assemblages of things: Drinking practices and inter-cultural interaction between Rhodes and Cyprus in the Late Bronze Age. In G. Bourogiannis, ed., *Beyond Cyprus: Investigating Cypriot Connectivity in the Mediterranean from the Late Bronze Age to the End of the Classical Period.* Athens: National and Kapodistrian University of Athens, pp. 225–37.

Smith, J. (2022). Cypriot seals and Cypriots overseas. In G. Bourogiannis, ed., *Beyond Cyprus: Investigating Cypriot Connectivity in the Mediterranean from the Late Bronze Age to the End of the Classical Period.* Athens: National and Kapodistrian University of Athens, pp. 207–23.

Snodgrass, A. (1971). *The Dark Age in Greece: An Archaeological Survey of the Eleventh to the Eighth Centuries BC.* Edinburgh: University of Edinburgh Press.

Snodgrass, A. (1991). Bronze Age exchange: A minimalist position. In N. Gale, ed., *Bronze Age Trade in the Mediterranean.* Jonsered: P. Åströms Verlag, pp. 15–21.

Sørensen, A. (2009). Approaching Levantine shores: Aspects of Cretan contacts with western Asia during the MM–LM I periods. In E. Hallager & S. Riisager, eds., *Proceedings of the Danish Institute at Athens VI.* Athens: Danish Institute at Athens, pp. 9–55.

Sowada, K., Newman, R., Albarède, F., et al. (2023). Analysis of Queen Hetepheres' bracelets from her celebrated tomb in Giza reveals new information on silver, metallurgy, and trade in Old Kingdom Egypt, c. 2600 BC. *Journal of Archaeological Science: Reports* **49**, 103978.

Spondylis, E. (2012). A Minoan shipwreck off Laconia. *Enalia* **11**, 6–7.

Stavropoulou-Gatsi, M., Jung, R., & Mehofer, M. (2012). Τάφος Μυκηναίου Πολεμιστή στον Κουβαρά Αιτωλοακαρνανίας. Πρώτη Παρουσίαση. In N.

Stampolidis, A. Kanta, & A. Giannikouri, eds., *The Earthly, The Celestial, and the Underworld in the Mediterranean from the Late Bronze and Early Iron Age.* Heraklion: University of Crete, pp. 249–66.

Steel, L. (2004). A reappraisal of the distribution, context, and function of Mycenaean pottery in Cyprus. *La Céramique Mycénienne de l'Égée au Levant, Travaux de la Maison de l'Orient et de la Méditerranée* **41**, 69–85.

Steel, L. (2013). *Materiality and Consumption in the Bronze Age Mediterranean.* London: Routledge.

Stockhammer, P. (2008). Kontinuität und Wandel: Die Keramik der Nachpalastzeit aus der Understadt von Tiryns. PhD dissertation. Ruprecht-Karls-Universität Heidelberg.

Stockhammer, P. (2015). Levantine and Cypriot pottery in Mycenaean Greece as mirrors of intercultural contacts. In A. Babbi, F. Bubenheimer-Erhart, B. Marín-Aguilera, & S. Mühl, eds., *The Mediterranean Mirror: Cultural Contacts in the Mediterranean Sea between 1200 and 750 BC.* Mainz: Verlagdes Römisch-Germanischen Zentralmuseums, pp. 177–88.

Stockhammer, P. (2020). The Aegean-type pottery from Tel Nami. In A. Gilboa & A. Yasur-Landau, eds., *Nomads of the Mediterranean,* Leiden: Brill, pp. 278–99.

Stos-Gale, Z. (2011). Biscuits with ears: A search for the origin of the earliest oxhide ingots. In P. Betancourt & S. Ferrence, eds., *Metallurgy: Understanding How, Learning Why.* Philadelphia: INSTAP, pp. 221–29.

Stos-Gale, Z. A., G. Maliotis, N. H. Gale, & N. Annetts. 1997. Lead Isotope Characteristics of the Cyprus Copper Ore Deposits Applied to Provenance Studies of Copper Oxhide Ingots. *Archaemetry* **39**, 83–123.

Stos-Gale, Z. (2014). Silver vessels in the Mycenaean Shaft Graves and their origin in the context of the metal supply in the Bronze Age Aegean. In H. Meller, R. Risch, & E. Pernicka, eds., *Metalle der Macht: Frühers Gold und Silber.* Halle: Landesmuseum für Vorgeschichte, pp. 183–208.

Tartaron, T. (2013). *Maritime Networks in the Mycenaean World.* Cambridge: Cambridge University Press.

Tartaron, T. (2018). Geography matters: Defining maritime small worlds of the Aegean Bronze Age. In J. Leidwanger & C. Knappett, eds., *Maritime Networks in the Ancient Mediterranean World.* Cambridge: Cambridge University Press, pp. 61–92.

Tomlinson, J., Rutter, J., & Hoffmann, S. (2010). Mycenaean and Cypriot Late Bronze Age ceramic imports to Kommos: An investigation by neutron activation analysis. *Hesperia* **79(2)**, 191–231.

Torrence, R. (1984). Monopoly or direct access? Industrial organization at the Melos obsidian quarries. In J. Ericson & B. Purdy, eds., *Prehistoric Quarries and Lithic Production.* Cambridge: Cambridge University Press, pp. 49–64.

Tournavitou, I. (1995). *The "Ivory Houses" at Mycenae*. Athens: British School at Athens.

Tsampiri, M. (2018). Obsidian in the prehistoric Aegean: Trade and uses. *Bulletin of the Geological Society of Greece* **53**, 28–49.

Van de Moortel, A. (2017). A new typology of Bronze Age Aegean ships: Developments in Aegean shipbuilding in their historical context. In J. Litwin, ed., *Baltic and Beyond: Change and Continuity in Shipbuilding*. Gdańsk: National Maritime Museum, pp. 263–68.

Van den Berg, K. (2018). Keeping in touch in a changing world: Network dynamics and the connections between the Aegean and Italy during the Bronze Age-Iron Age transition (ca. 1250–1000 BC). PhD Dissertation. Vrije University of Amsterdam.

Varberg, J., Gratuze, B., Kaul, F., et al. (2016). Mesopotamian glass from Late Bronze Age Egypt, Romania, Germany, and Denmark. *Journal of Archaeological Science* **74**, 184–94.

Vavouranakis, G. (2020). The mechanics of cultural hybridization in the southern Aegean during the third millennium BC. *Journal of Eastern Mediterranean Archaeology and Heritage Studies* **8(3–4)**, 299–313.

Vetters, M. (2011). A clay ball with a Cypro-Minoan inscription from Tiryns. *Archäologischer Anzeiger* **2011(2)**, 1–49.

Vetters, M., & Weilhartner, J. (2017). A nude man is hard to find: Tracing the development of Mycenaean late palatial iconography for a male deity. *Mitteilungen des Deutschen Archäologischen Instituts: Athenische Abteilung* **131/132**, 31–78.

Viglietti, C. (2021). Cultural hegemonies, "NIE-orthodoxy", and social development models. Classicists' "organic" approaches to economic history in the early XXI century. In E. Zucchetti & A.-M. Cimino, eds., *Antonio Gramsci and the Ancient World*. London: Routledge, pp. 301–26.

Vitale, S., & Trecarichi, A. (2015). The Koan tradition during the Mycenaean Age: A contextual and functional analysis of local ceramics from the "Serraglio", Eleona, and Langada. In N. Stampolidis, Ç. Maner, & K. Kopanias, eds., *NOSTOI: Indigenous Culture, Migration + Integration in the Aegean Islands + Western Anatolia during the Late Bronze and Early Iron Ages*. Istanbul: Koç University Press, pp. 311–35.

Vlachopoulos, A. (2012). *Η Υστεροελλαδική ΙΙΙΓ περίοδος στη Νάξο: Τα ταφικά σύνολα και οι συσχετισμοί τους με το Αιγαίο*, vol. 2. Athens: University of Athens.

Vlachopoulos, A., & Georgiadis, M. (2015). The Cyclades and the Dodecanese during the Post-palatial period. In N. Stampolidis, Ç. Maner, & K. Kopanias, eds., *NOSTOI: Indigenous Culture, Migration + Integration in the Aegean*

Islands + Western Anatolia during the Late Bronze and Early Iron Ages. Istanbul: Koç University Press, pp. 337–68.

Voskos, I., & Knapp, A. B. (2008). Cyprus at the end of the Late Bronze Age: Crisis and colonization, or continuity and hybridization? *American Journal of Archaeology* **112**, 659–84.

Voutsaki, S. (2001). Economic control, power, and prestige in the Mycenaean world: The archaeological evidence. In S. Voutsaki & J. Killen, eds., *Economy and Politics in the Mycenaean Palace States.* Cambridge: Cambridge Philological Society, pp. 195–213.

Walberg, G. (1988). Kamares imitations in Egypt and their social and economic implications. In J. Christiansen & T. Melander, eds., *Proceedings of the 3rd Symposium on Ancient Greek and Related Pottery.* Copenhagen: Ny Carlsberg Glyptotek, pp. 634–39.

Warburton, D., ed. (2022). *The Earliest Economic Growth in World History: Proceedings of the Berlin Workshop.* Leuven: Peeters.

Warren, P. (1969). *Minoan Stone Vases.* Cambridge: Cambridge University Press.

Warren, P. (2000). Crete and Egypt: The transmission of relationships. In A. Karetsou, ed., *Kriti-Aigyptos*, vol. 1. Heraklion: Archaeological Museum of Heraklion, pp. 24–28.

Watrous, V. (1998). Egypt and Crete in the Early Middle Bronze Age: A case of trade and cultural diffusion. In E. Cline & D. Harris-Cline, eds., *The Aegean and the Orient in the Second Millennium.* Liège: University of Liège, pp. 19–28.

Weingarten, J. (2000). Early Helladic II sealings from Geraki in Lakonia: Evidence for property, textile manufacture, and trade. In I. Pini, ed., *Minoisch-Mykenische Glyptik. Stil, Ikonographie, Funktion.* Berlin: Gebr. Mann Verlag, pp. 317–29.

Wilson, D. (1999). *Ayia Irini: Periods I–III: The Neolithic and Early Bronze Age Settlements: Part 1: The Pottery and Small Finds: Keos IX.* Mainz am Rhein: Philipp von Zabern.

Wood, J., Hsu, Y.-T., & Bell, C. (2021). Sending Laurion back to the future: Bronze Age silver and the source of confusion. *Internet Archaeology* **56**, 9.

Woudhuizen, F. (2017). Towards a reconstruction of tin-trade routes in Mediterranean protohistory. *Praehistorische Zeitschrift* **92**, 342–53.

Yahalom-Mack, N., Galili, E., Segal, I., et al. (2014). New insights into Levantine copper trade: Analysis of ingots from the Bronze and Iron Ages in Israel. *Journal of Archaeological Science* **45**, 159–77.

Zaccagnini, C. (1983). Patterns of mobility among ancient Near Eastern craftsmen. *Journal of Near Eastern Studies* **42**(4), 245–64.

Zachos, K. (2010). Η Μεταλλουργία στην Ελλάδα και στη ΝΑ Ευρώπη κατά την 5$^\eta$ και 4$^\eta$ χιλιετία π.Χ. In N. Papadimitriou & Z. Tsirtsoni, eds., *Η Ελλάδα στο ευρύτερο πολιτισμικό πλαίσιο των Βαλκανίων κατά την 5$^\eta$ και 4$^\eta$ χιλιετία π.Χ.* Athens: N. P Goulandris Institute, pp. 77–91.

Zachos, K., & Dousougli, A. (2008). Observations on the Early Bronze Age sealings from the Cave of Zas at Naxos. In N. Brodie, J. Doole, G. Gavalas, & C. Renfrew, eds., *Horizon – Ορίζων: A Colloquium on the Prehistory of the Cyclades*. Cambridge: McDonald Institute of Archaeology, pp. 85–95.

Zangani, F. (2016). Amarna and Uluburun: Reconsidering patterns of exchange in the Late Bronze Age. *Palestine Exploration Quarterly* **148(4)**, 230–44.

Zervaki, F. (2022). From Cyprus to Rhodes and beyond: Cypriot imports and influence in Rhodes in the 11th and early 10th centuries BC: Links to the Aegean and the Central Mediterranean. In G. Bourogiannis, ed., *Beyond Cyprus: Investigating Cypriot Connectivity in the Mediterranean from the Late Bronze Age to the End of the Classical Period*. Athens: National and Kapodistrian University of Athens, pp. 239–50.

Zuckerman, S., Bechar, S., Ben-Shlomo, D., Mommsen, H., & Mountjoy, P. (2020). Neutron activation analysis of Mycenaean pottery from north Israel: Reconstruction of Aegean-Levantine trade patterns. *Ägypten und Levante* **30**, 569–633.

Cambridge Elements

Aegean Bronze Age

Carl Knappett

University of Toronto

Carl Knappett is the Walter Graham/ Homer Thompson Chair in Aegean Prehistory at the University of Toronto.

Irene Nikolakopoulou

Hellenic Ministry of Culture and Archaeological Museum of Heraklion

Irene Nikolakopoulou is an archaeologist and curator at the Archaeological Museum of Heraklion, Crete.

About the Series

This series is devised thematically to foreground the conceptual developments in the Aegean Bronze Age, one of the richest subfields of archaeology, while reflecting the range of institutional settings in which research in this field is conducted. It aims to produce an innovative and comprehensive review of the latest scholarship in Aegean prehistory.

Cambridge Elements ⹀

Aegean Bronze Age

Elements in the Series